DYNAMICS—THE GEOMETRY OF BEHAVIOR

PART 4: BIFURCATION BEHAVIOR

VISMATH: THE VISUAL MATHEMATICS LIBRARY
VOLUME 4

The Visual Mathematics Library
Ralph H. Abraham, Editor

VISMATH BOOKS:

VOLUME 1: Abraham and Shaw, DYNAMICS—THE GEOMETRY OF BEHAVIOR
Part 1: Periodic Behavior

VOLUME 2: Abraham and Shaw, DYNAMICS—THE GEOMETRY OF BEHAVIOR
Part 2: Chaotic Behavior

VOLUME 3: Abraham and Shaw, DYNAMICS—THE GEOMETRY OF BEHAVIOR
Part 3: Global Behavior

VOLUME 4: Abraham and Shaw, DYNAMICS—THE GEOMETRY OF BEHAVIOR
Part 4: Bifurcation Behavior

VISMATH COMPUTER GRAPHIC PROGRAMS:

DISK 1: Abraham and Norskog, PHASE PORTRAITS IN THE PLANE

DISK 2: Abraham and Norskog, CHAOTIC ATTRACTORS IN 3D

VISMATH LIBRARY FILMS:

FILM 1: Stewart, THE LORENZ SYSTEM

FILM 2: Roux, Shaw, and Swinney, STRANGE ATTRACTOR IN A CHEMICAL SYSTEM

FILM 3: Crutchfield, CHAOTIC ATTRACTORS OF DRIVEN OSCILLATORS

VISMATH LIBRARY VIDEOS:

TAPE 1: Langton, ARTIFICIAL LIFE

TAPE 2: Crutchfield, VIDEO FEEDBACK

SERIES FOREWORD

During the Renaissance, algebra was resumed from Near Eastern sources, and geometry from the Greek. Scholars of the time became familiar with classical mathematics. When calculus was born in 1665, the new ideas spread quickly through the intellectual circles of Europe. Our history shows the importance of the diffusion of these mathematical ideas, and their effects upon the subsequent development of the sciences and technology.

Today, there is a cultural resistance to mathematical ideas. Due to the widespread impression that mathematics is difficult to understand, or to a structural flaw in our educational system, or perhaps to other mechanisms, mathematics has become an esoteric subject. Intellectuals of all sorts now carry on their discourse in nearly total ignorance of mathematical ideas. We cannot help thinking that this is a critical situation, as we hold the view that mathematical ideas are essential for the future evolution of our society.

The absence of visual representations in the curriculum may be part of the problem, contributing to mathematical illiteracy, and to the math-avoidance reflex. This series is based on the idea that mathematical concepts may be communicated easily in a format which combines visual, verbal, and symbolic representations in tight coordination. It aims to attack math ignorance with an abundance of visual representations.

In sum, the purpose of this series is to encourage the diffusion of mathematical ideas, by presenting them *visually*.

THE VISUAL MATHEMATICS LIBRARY: VISMATH VOLUME 4

DYNAMICS — THE GEOMETRY OF BEHAVIOR

Part 4: Bifurcation Behavior

with 201 illustrations

by

Ralph H. Abraham

and

Christopher D. Shaw

University of California
Santa Cruz, CA 95064

Aerial Press, Inc.
P.O.Box 1360, Santa Cruz, California, 95061

First Printing, 5000 copies, October 1988

Library of Congress Cataloging in Publication Data
Library of Congress Catalog Card Number: 81-71616
ISBN 0-942344-04-9 (Volume 4)
ISBN 0-942344-00-6 (four volume set)

Original text reproduced by Aerial Press, Inc., from camera ready copy prepared by the authors.
All final drawings and color separations by Diane Rigoli. Copyright by Aerial Press, Inc., 1988.

Printed in the United States of America.

CONTENTS

Preface to the Dynamics Books

what is dynamics?

___

Dynamics is a field emerging somewhere between mathematics and the sciences. In our view, it is the most exciting event on the concept horizon for many years. The new concepts appearing in dynamics extend the conceptual power of our civilization, and provide new understanding in many fields.

the visual math format

___

We discovered, while working together on the illustrations for a book in 1978, that we could explain mathematical ideas visually, within an easy and pleasant working partnership. In 1980, we wrote an expository article on dynamics and bifurcations using hand-animation to emulate the *dynamic picture technique* universally used by mathematicians in talking among themselves: a picture is drawn slowly, line-by-line, along with a spoken narrative — the dynamic picture and the narrative tightly coordinated.

Our efforts inevitably exploded into four volumes of this series, of which this is the fourth. The dynamic picture technique, evolved through our work together, and in five years of computer graphic experience with the *Visual Math Project* at the University of California at Santa Cruz, is the basis of this work. About two-thirds of the books are devoted to visual representations, in which colors are used according to a strict code.

Moving versions of the phase portraits, *actual dynamic pictures,* will be made available as *computer graphic programs* on floppy disks for home computers, and as *videotapes, videodiscs, or films.*

on the suppression of symbols

___

Math symbols have been kept to a minimum. In fact, they are almost completely suppressed. Our purpose is to make the book work for readers who are not practiced in symbolic representations. We rely exclusively on visual representations, with brief verbal explanations. Some formulas are shown with the applications, as part of the graphics, but are not essential. However, *this strategy is exclusively pedagogic.* We do not want anyone to think that we consider symbolic representations unimportant in mathematics. On the contrary, this field evolved primarily in the symbolic realm throughout the classical period. Even now, a full understanding of our subject demands a full measure of formulas, logical expressions, and technical intricacies from all branches of mathematics. Brief introductions to these are included as appendices to *Part One, Periodic Behavior,* and *Part Two, Chaotic Behavior.*

our goals

We have created these books as a short-cut to the research frontier of dynamical systems: theory, experiments, and applications. It is our goal—we know we may fail to reach it—to provide any interested person with an acquaintance with the basic concepts:

* state spaces: manifolds—geometric models for the virtual states of a system
* attractors: static, periodic, and chaotic—geometric models for its local asymptotic behavior
* separatrices: repellors, saddles, insets, tangles—defining the boundaries of regions (basins) dominated by different behaviors (attractors), and characterizing the global behavior of a system
* bifurcations: subtle and catastrophic—geometric models for the controlled change of one system into another.

The ideas included are selected from the literature of dynamics: *Part 1, Periodic Behavior,* covers the classical period from 1600 to 1950. (These are needed for all the following volumes.) *Part 2, Chaotic Behavior,* is devoted to recent developments, 1950 to the present, on the chaotic behavior observed in experiments. *Part 3, Global Behavior,* describes the concept of structural stability, discovered in 1937, and the important generic properties discovered since 1959, relating to the tangled insets and outsets of a dynamical system. These are fundamental to this volume, *Part 4, Bifurcation Behavior,* which will complete the sequence, *Dynamics, the Geometry of Behavior.* In fact, the presentation in this volume of an atlas of bifurcations in dynamical schemes with one control parameter was the original and primary goal of this whole series, and all of the topics in the preceding volumes have been selected for their importance to the understanding of these bifurcations. For we regard the *response diagram,* a molecular arrangement of the atomic bifurcation events described here, as the most useful dynamical model available to a scientist.

prerequisite background

We assume nothing in the way of prior mathematical training, beyond vectors in three dimensions, and complex numbers. Nevertheless, it will be tough going without a basic understanding of the simplest concepts of calculus. All the essential ideas will be presented in *Volume 0* of this series.

acknowledgements

Our first attempt at the pictorial style used here evolved in the first draft of *Dynamics, a Visual Introduction,* during the Summer of 1980. Our next effort, the preliminary draft of Volume 2 of this series, was circulated among friends in the Summer of 1981. Extensive feedback from them has been very influential in the evolution of this volume, and the whole series, and we are grateful to them:

Fred Abraham	George Francis	Nelson Max	Rob Shaw
Ethan Akin	Alan Garfinkel	Jerry Marsden	Mike Shub
Michael Arbib	John Guckenheimer	Jim McGill	Steve Smale
Jim Crutchfield	Moe Hirsch	Kent Morrison	Joel Smoller
Larry Cuba	Phil Holmes	Charles Muse	Jim Swift
Richard Cushman	Dan Joseph	Norman Packard	Bob Williams
Larry Domash	Jean-Michel Kantor	Tim Poston	Art Winfree
Jean-Pierre Eckman	Bob Lansdon	Otto Rössler	Marianne Wolpert
Len Fellman	Arnold Mandell	Lee Rudolph	Gene Yates
		Katie Scott	Chris Zeeman

We are especially grateful to Tim Poston and Fred Abraham for their careful reading of the manuscript, to Claire Moore and Phyllis Wright of TypaGraphix for their care in the layout of the book using text transposed from Macintosh to a Compugraphic digital phototypesetter, to Laura Lato of Aerial Press for her expert assistance in the production process, to Diane Rigoli for her splendid final drawings based on our rough sketches, and to Rob Shaw for providing photos for Section 1.3 and computer plots for Section 2.3. The generosity and goodwill of many dynamicists has been crucial in the preparation of this book; we thank them all. Finally, we are grateful to Tom Jones, André Leroi-Gourhan, Preston James, Goeffrey Martin and their publishers for permitting the reproduction of their illustrations.

Ralph H. Abraham
Christopher D. Shaw
Santa Cruz, California
August, 1988

dedicated to
René Thom

Photograph by Ismael Selim Khaznadar.

DYNAMICS
THE GEOMETRY OF BEHAVIOR

Part Four: Bifurcation Behavior

BIFURCATION HALL OF FAME

Bifurcation concepts emerged early in the history of dynamics. Soon after Newton the first case, the pitchfork, was discovered. Eventually, bifurcation theory bifurcated into two branches, dealing with similar phenomena in the contexts of ordinary differential equations (ODEs) and partial differential equations (PDEs), respectively. ODEs comprise the type of model introduced by Newton for mechanics, and this has evolved in this century into dynamical systems theory. PDEs were introduced by d'Alembert in 1749 to model the continuous (that is, spatially extended) mechanics of the vibrating string.

Recently, thanks to global analysis, these two branches have reunited. This reunification bifurcation was effected by reinterpreting a PDE in a finite-dimensional physical space as an ODE in an infinite-dimensional space of functions. In this section we give capsule biographies of some of the historically important personalities. Further description of their roles in the history of the subject may be found in Chapter 1.

TABLE 1. THE HISTORY OF BIFURCATION THEORY		
Date	ODE	PDE
1600		
		Hooke Newton
1700		Clairaut Maclaurin Simpson d'Alembert
1800		Jacobi
1900	Poincaré Liapounov Andronov Hopf Thom	Tchebychev Liapounov Poincaré Couette Taylor
2000		

Here are some capsule histories.

Robert Hooke, 1635-1703. In 1683, Hooke guessed that the Earth was flattened at the poles.

Isaac Newton, 1642-1727. In 1687, Newton asssumed that the Earth was a spheroid, flattened at the poles. To calculate its eccentricity, he devised his *principle of canals.*

Alexis Claude Clairaut, 1713-1765. Clairaut examined the possibility that Newton's oblate spheroid was a relative equilibrium for a blob of fluid.

Colin Maclaurin, 1698-1746. Using Newton's principle of canals, he established, in 1742, the relative equilibrium of a rotating ellipsoid of homogeneous fluid, subsequently known as a *Maclaurin spheroid.*

Thomas Simpson, 1710-1761. By careful analysis, he actually showed in 1743 that *two distinct Maclaurin spheroids* were relative equilibra, implying a bifurcation in the possible figures of the earth.

Jean d'Alembert, 1717-1783. He explicitly analysed, in 1768, the bifurcation implied by Simpson in 1743.

Carl Gustav Jakob Jacobi, 1804-1851. In 1834, he discovered a new equilibrium figure for a rotating fluid blob, the *Jacobi ellipsoid.* Also, he introduced the word *bifurcation* in this context, to describe the relationship between the Maclaurin spheroids and the ellipsoidal figures.

Jules Henri Poincaré, 1854-1912. The question of the *stability* of the figures of the earth was introduced by Poincaré in 1885, in response to a problem posed in 1882 by Tchebychev on the evolution of the figure in the case of a gradually increasing angular momentum. He also carried over this concept into our current context of dynamical systems.

Aleksandr Mikhailovich Liapounov, 1857-1918. Liapounov considered the problem of Tchebychev also, and created his classical theory of stability in this context.

Aleksandr Aleksandrovich Andronov, 1901-1952. Andronov created a complete theory of bifurcations of dynamical systems in the plane.

Eberhard Hopf. Published, in 1942, a rigorous proof of the first excitation event, after which it became known as the *Hopf bifurcation.*

René Thom. The publication of Thom's revolutionary book, *Structural Stability and Morphogenesis,* in 1972 marked a major turning point in the importance of nonlinear dynamics and bifurcation theory to the sciences: physical, biological, and social. Without doubt he is the most important pioneer in this area since Poincaré and we are all deeply in his debt. In recognition of this, we have dedicated this volume to him.

1. Origins of Bifurcation Concepts

In *Part One, Periodic Behavior,* limit points and cycles in dimensions one, two, and three were introduced. The decomposition of the state space into basins of attraction, by the separatrices, was emphasized. In *Part Two, Chaotic Behavior,* the inset structure of the separatrices was developed. The geometry of the exceptional limit sets, determined by their Lyapounov characteristic exponents, was described. In *Part Three, Global Behavior,* the fundamental idea of structural stability was introduced, along with the related notion of generic property.

All of this material is basic to the theory, experiments, and applications of dynamics. However, the most important of all, from the point of view of applications, are the *bifurcations of* dynamical systems being changed by a control parameter. This is the subject of this volume, and in the preceding volumes we have selected topics so as to create the minimum background needed for this theory.

In this chapter, we trace the history of the bifurcation concept from darkest antiquity.

1.1. THE BATTLE OF THE BULGE

Our knowledge of the shape of the Earth has grown throughout history, and out of this history emerged the concepts of bifurcation theory. We begin with a capsule version of this story. A splendid 150 page version may be found in Jones [1]. For the associated mathematical details, consult Todhunter [2].

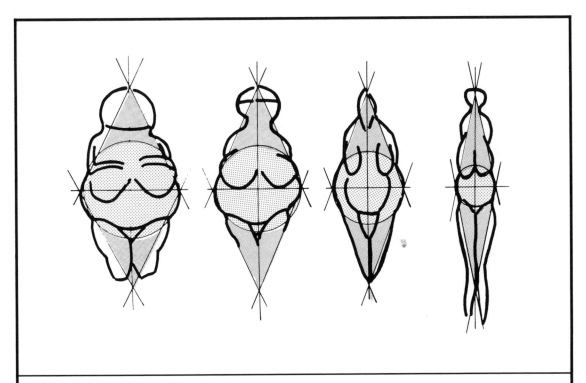

1.1.1. The Earth, Gaia, Goddess: what is her figure? The Venus figurine from the Gravettian culture, found throughout Upper Paleolithic Europe, is generally assumed to be a fertility amulet. (Reproduced from Leroi-Gourhan.) Was it also a geographical model of the Earth?

We do not know when or how the globular shape of our home planet was first discovered, but we do know that Aristotle knew it by 350 BCE. And by 225 BCE, Eratosthenes (the Alexandrian librarian) knew its circumference within one percent! Thus begins the early history of our subject. Things changed little until the dawn of the Baroque, although confidence in Eratosthenes had waned by the time of Columbus.

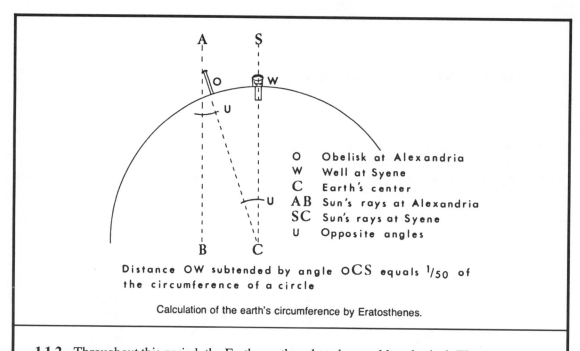

O   Obelisk at Alexandria
W   Well at Syene
C   Earth's center
AB   Sun's rays at Alexandria
SC   Sun's rays at Syene
U   Opposite angles

Distance OW subtended by angle OCS equals $^1/_{50}$ of the circumference of a circle

Calculation of the earth's circumference by Eratosthenes.

1.1.2. Throughout this period, the Earth was thought to be roughly spherical. Then paradoxes began to accumulate.

One problem was the discrepancies in the measurements of the circumference, some of which were done with great care. Another difficulty was the accuracy of pendulum clocks, which were found to slow down at the equator. Here is a summary of the events casting doubt on the spherical hypothesis.

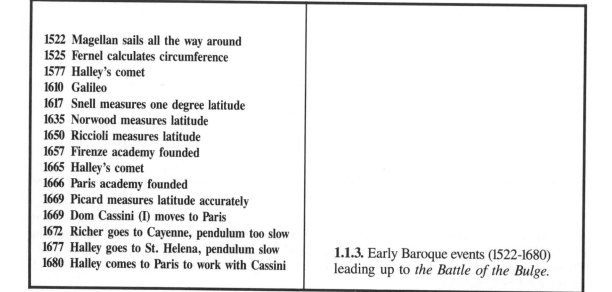

1522 Magellan sails all the way around
1525 Fernel calculates circumference
1577 Halley's comet
1610 Galileo
1617 Snell measures one degree latitude
1635 Norwood measures latitude
1650 Riccioli measures latitude
1657 Firenze academy founded
1665 Halley's comet
1666 Paris academy founded
1669 Picard measures latitude accurately
1669 Dom Cassini (I) moves to Paris
1672 Richer goes to Cayenne, pendulum too slow
1677 Halley goes to St. Helena, pendulum slow
1680 Halley comes to Paris to work with Cassini

1.1.3. Early Baroque events (1522-1680) leading up to *the Battle of the Bulge*.

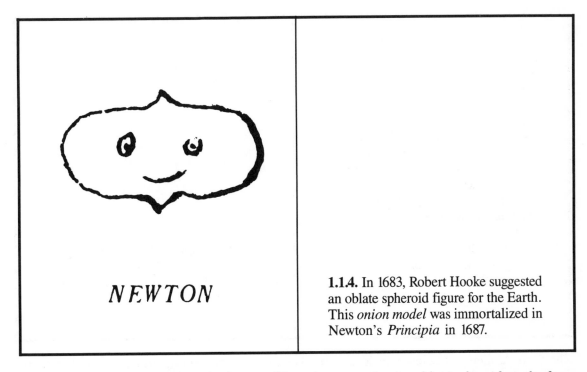

NEWTON

1.1.4. In 1683, Robert Hooke suggested an oblate spheroid figure for the Earth. This *onion model* was immortalized in Newton's *Principia* in 1687.

A *spheroid* is what you get by spinning an ellipse about an axis. An *oblate spheroid* results from spinning around the shorter axis. A spanish onion or a bun has this shape. A *prolate spheriod* results from spinning around the longer (major) axis. A lemon has this shape. An *ellipsoid* is not made by spinning, but has elliptical sections when cut.

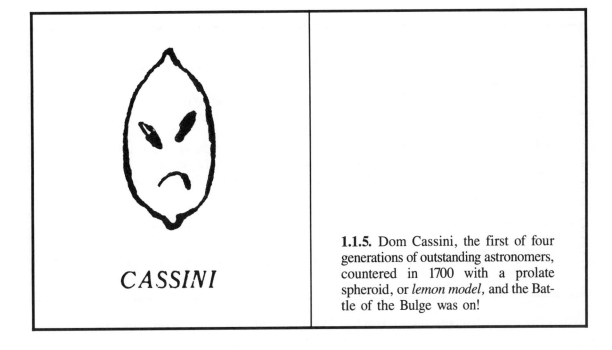

CASSINI

1.1.5. Dom Cassini, the first of four generations of outstanding astronomers, countered in 1700 with a prolate spheroid, or *lemon model,* and the Battle of the Bulge was on!

1683 Robert Hooke makes onion
      hypothesis
1685 J. S. Bach born
1686 Fontenelle publishes 'Plurality of
      Worlds,' popularising Descartes
1687 Isaac Newton publishes onion
      hypothesis with mechanical
      arguments, computations
1690 Huyghens supports Newton
1691 Dom Cassini observes oblateness
      of Jupiter
1700 Dom Cassini publishes the
      lemon hypothesis

1.1.6. The events (1680-1700) leading up to the controversy, which nearly resulted in World War in Europe and the Americas.

The Paris Academy of Science decided to resolve the crisis by sending expeditions to the Arctic Circle in Lapland and to the Equator in Ecuador, to make definitive measurements of meridianal arcs of one degree of latitude. These would be North to South arcs of about 110.5 kilometers (68.7 miles) length, assuming a spherical figure. Between endpoints determined by observing the angle to the Sun at noon (as in celestial navigation), the measured length should be longer than 110.5 kilometers for a prolate spheroid, and shorter for an oblate one.

1718   Jacques Cassini publishes measurements supporting the lemon hypothesis
1727   Newton died
1732   Maupertuis and Clairaut support Newton's onion hypothesis
1733   La Condamine proposes expedition to Equator (Cayenne)
1734   Godin suggests expedition to Equator (Ecuador)
1735   Expedition leaves Paris for Ecuador with La Condamine and Bouguer
        Maupertuis proposes expedition to Arctic Circle (Lapland)
1736   Expedition leaves Paris for Lapland with Maupertuis, Clairaut, and
        Celsius

1.1.7. Here, in a nutshell, is the sequence of events during the early years of the conflict, 1718-1736.

When the measurements finally reached Paris in 1744, the onion team had won.

1737 Lapland measurements reach Paris

Algarotti publishes popular account of Newton's optics

D. Bernoulli analyzes fluid cylinder

1738 Clairaut finds a formula for the equilibrium of a rotating fluid blob

Euler writes analysis of the fluid onion

1739 War of Jenkins' ear, and pyramids

1740 Maclaurin proves the onion for a rotating blob of homogeneous fluid

Cassini publishes new measurements supporting the lemon hypothesis

1743 Expedition leaves Ecuador for home

1744 Bouguer arrives in Paris

Ecuador measurements completed by La Condamine and Bouguer

Maupertuis finds the principle of least action

d'Alembert analyses the fluid blob

Celsius dies

Cassini de Thury capitulates

La Condamine returns to Paris

1750 J. S. Bach dies

1759 Halley's comet

1.1.8. The last eight years of battle, during which hydrostatics and bifurcation theory were born.

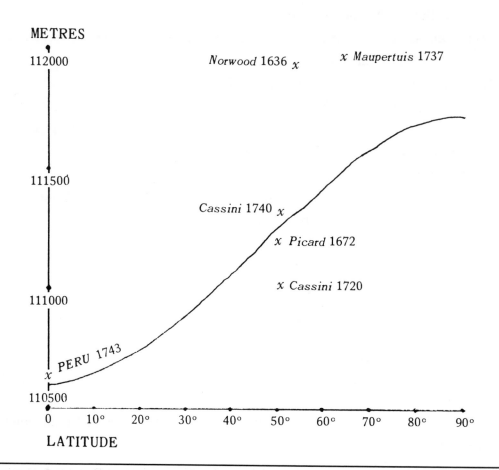

Degree of Latitude in Meters compared with early measures
(after *Geographical Journal* 98 (1941) p. 292)

1.1.9. Here is a summary display of the best known measurements of a one degree arc, taken from the Geographical Journal [3]. The measures at all latitudes would fall along a horizontal line, if the world were spherical. The rise toward the pole (on the right) confirms an prolate (onion) figure.

			1600	1700	1800
Cassini I	1625	1712			
Huyghens	1629	1695			
Newton	1642	1727			
Bach	1685	1750			
Bouguer	1698	1758			
Maupertuis	1698	1759			
Maclaurin	1698	1746			
La Condamine	1701	1774			
Clairaut	1713	1765			
Cassini II	1677	1756			
Euler	1707	1783			
Simpson	1710	1761			
Clairaut	1713	1765			
Cassini III	1714	1784			
d'Alembert	1717	1783			
Lagrange	1736	1813			
Cassini IV	1748	1845			
Laplace	1749	1827			

1.1.10. The cast of characters in order of their appearance.

We turn now to the emergence, in this strange context, of the bifurcation concepts which are fundamental to the modern theory of bifurcation behavior.

1.2 THE FIGURE OF THE EARTH

From this amazing story of scientific conflict and creativity which dominated the activities of the first scientific societies of Europe throughout their early years, we here extract the mathematical events leading up to the development of the bifurcation concepts of modern dynamical systems theory. These considerations deal with a rotating homogeneous fluid mass (or *blob*) and apply equally to the cosmogenic problems of stellar evolution and galaxy formation. For additional details, see Hagihara [4] and Lyttleton [5].

From 400 BCE until 1683, the Earth was thought to be roughly spherical.

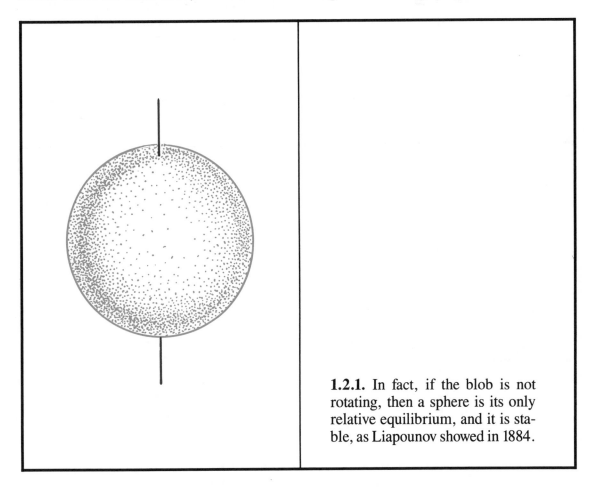

1.2.1. In fact, if the blob is not rotating, then a sphere is its only relative equilibrium, and it is stable, as Liapounov showed in 1884.

But it *is* rotating. Newton introduced the *principle of canals* in his *Principia* of 1687, to analyse the dynamics of a spinning oblate spheroid (onion shape).

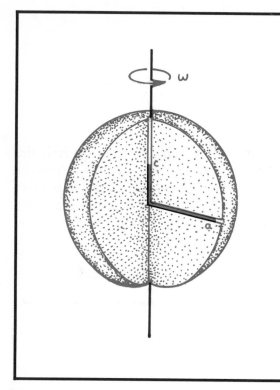

1.2.2. *The principle of canals.* In the spherical Earth, assumed solid, drill two long tunnels which meet in the center: one from the North Pole, and another from some point on the Equator. Fill nearly full with water. Due to the centrifugal force (named by Huyghens but successfully analysed by Newton as a graduate student) the Equatorial tube of water will be pulled outward, rising to a higher level than the polar tube.

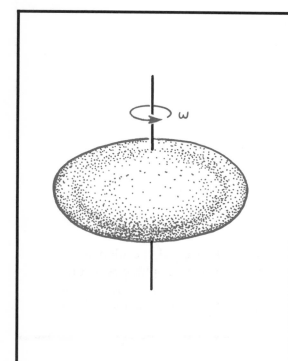

1.2.3. Using the principle of canals, Newton calculated the eccentricity needed by the onion (as a function of its angular momentum) to maintain equilibrium. Maclaurin proved this condition was necessary for hydrostatic equilibrium in 1740, and Clairaut generalized his result to inhomogeneous blobs.

The analysis of the onion by the principle of canals was completed by Simpson [6] in 1743. Let 2a denote the length of the major axis of an ellipse, 2b the length of the minor axis, and 2c the distance between its foci. Then $a^2 = b^2 + c^2$. Recall that the *eccentricity* of the ellipse is the ratio c/a. The ratio is zero for a circle, and is always less than one. A similar index was introduced by Clairaut to describe spheroids. Let 2A denote the equatorial diameter, and 2B denote the polar diameter. Then the *ellipticity* of the spheroid is the ratio $e = (A-B)/A$ as described in Todhunter. [7] The ellipticity is positive for a prolate (onion) spheroid, zero for a sphere, and negative for an oblate (lemon) spheroid.

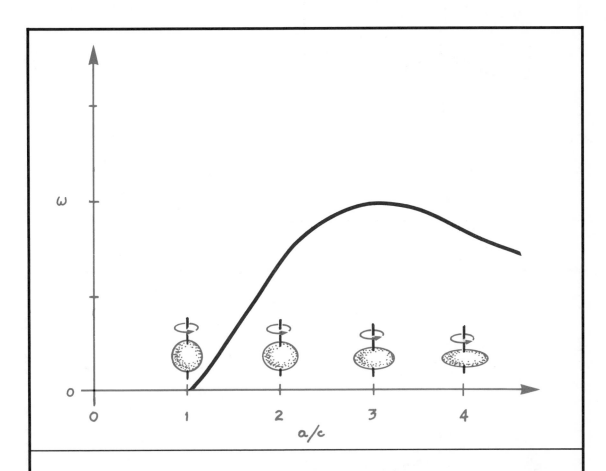

1.2.4. As the eccentricity of the homogeneous spheroidal blob increases, the angular velocity traces out this curve, obtained by Simpson, with a maximum at e = 0.9299, or B/A = 2.7198 [8], or E = - 1.7198 (a long lemon). Thus for smaller velocities there are two equilibrium Maclaurin spheroids having the same rate of rotation, and there is a maximum rate. However, the angular momentum goes on increasing along this curve [9], which describes the *Maclaurin series* of spheroids.

The next major advance in our story was the discovery by Jacobi in 1834 of a new figure which defies intuition, in that it does not have rotational symmetry.

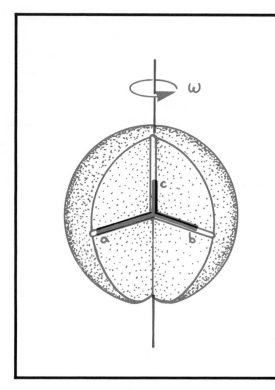

1.2.5. Drilling three canals in a spherical Earth, the two Equatorial canals would be expected to have the same equilibrium water level. Jacobi showed that this is not necessarily true.

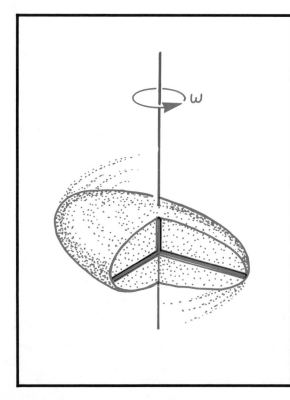

1.2.6. The rotating ellipsoids, with three unequal axes (rotating about the shortest of the three) will be in hydrostatic equilibrium at the correct rate of rotation. These are now called the *Jacobi ellipsoids*. They are found in a curve of increasing ellipticity, called the *Jacobi series* of ellipsoids.

The two series of equilibrium figures actually cross. That is, at one special case of the Maclaurin series, the Jacobi series *branches off* from the Maclaurin series.

It is for this crossing point that Jacobi invented the word bifurcation.

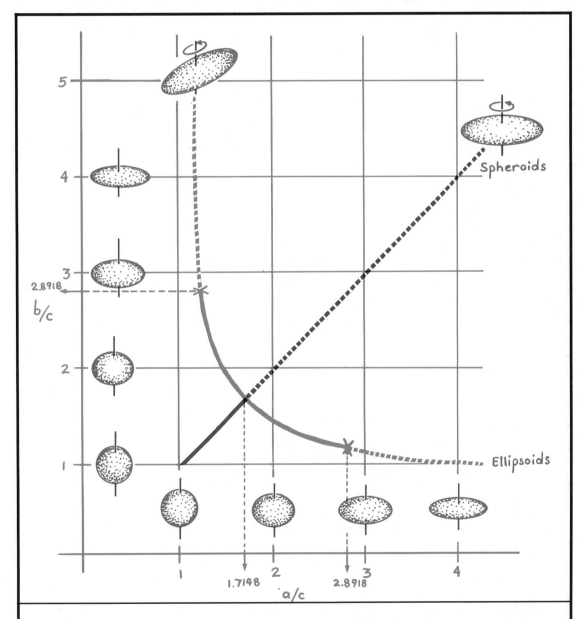

1.2.7. Here are the two series, Maclaurin in blue and Jacobi in red. The coordinates represent the diameters of the equatorial ellipse, if the polar diameter is taken as *one*. Note that the Maclaurin series occupies the diagonal, along which the two equatorial diameters are equal. That is, the spheroids are special cases of the ellipsoids [10].

In 1882 Tchebychev asked how the equilibrium figure changes as the angular momentum is gradually increased. This is the essential question in most applications of bifurcation theory today, and we may take this moment as the alpha point of the history of bifurcation theory.

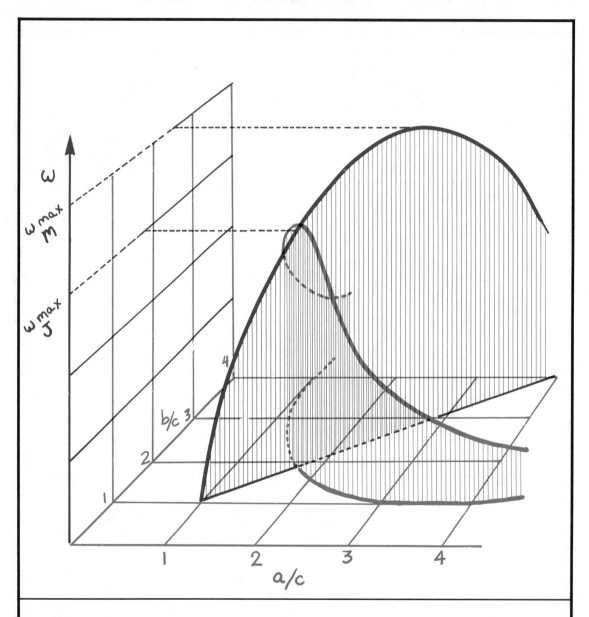

1.2.8. Adding angular velocity as a third (vertical) coordinate, the two crossing series are draped like this. The Maclaurin series (blue curve) has a maximum, as discovered by Simpson, and the Jacobi series also has a maximum velocity, but smaller than the Maclaurin maximum. This was discovered by Sir G. H. Darwin [11] in 1887.

Relative equilibria of a dynamical problem may be stable or unstable. The unstable ones, in general, will not be observed. Thus, the relevance of the mathematical models of Newton to the actual figures of the planets and stars will depend critically on stability.

And yet, the stability problem was never analysed until Poincaré and Liapounov attacked Tchebychev's problem in 1885. After forty years, the last part of the problem was resolved by Cartan [12] in 1922.

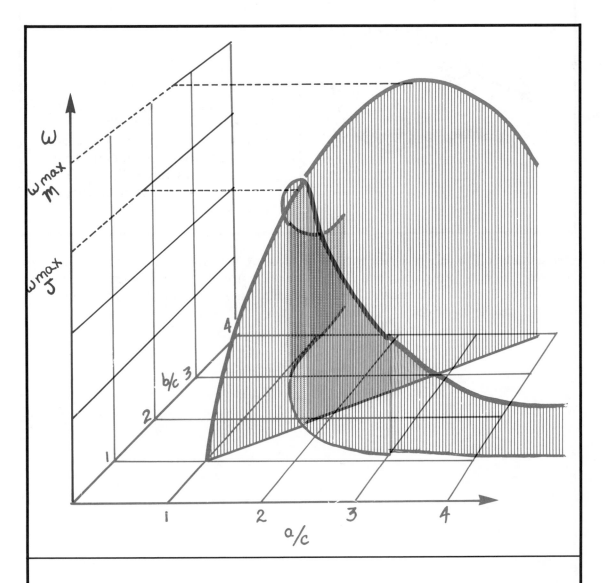

1.2.9. Here again is the plot of the two series, in the space of eccentricity and angular velocity, as before. But here, the stable branches are shown in red, the unstable ones in green.

This is the final stage in the emergence of the first bifurcation diagram in history, the *pitchfork*. But, there is more to our history of the figures of the Earth.

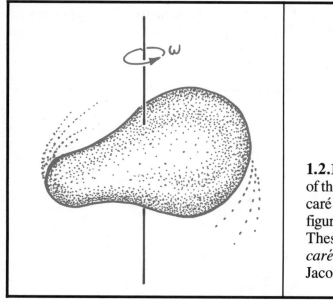

1.2.10. While studying the stability of the Jacobi series of equilibria, Poincaré discovered yet another equilibrium figure, the *pear-shape* or piriform figure. These occur in series, called the *Poincaré series,* which branch off from the Jacobi series.

The stability of the Jacobi series ends at its crossing with the Poincaré series. Poincaré believed the pears were stable, and could explain the origin of double stars and planetary satellites by a kind of hydrostatic bifurcation. But Liapounov was convinced they were unstable, and he was right.

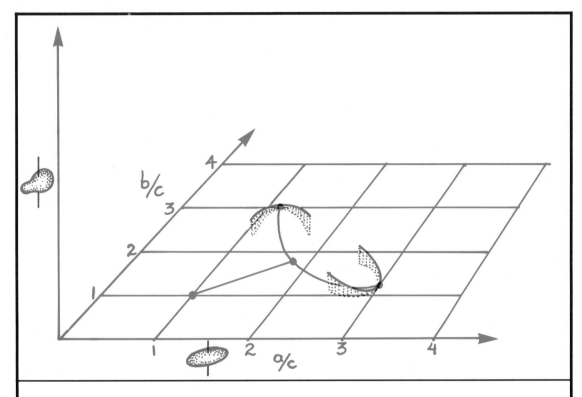

1.2.11. Here is a plot of the three series, showing stability in red. The horizontal axes are the overall ellipticity of the Equatorial section as before, while the vertical axis represents pearness. The arrival of the unstable branches of the Poincaré series at the Jacobi series kills its stability. This is an example of a *catastrophic* bifurcation, and is the related to the pitchfork bifurcation at the branching of the Jacobi series from the Maclaurin series.

Both of these historic bifurcation events were discovered by Poincaré [13] in 1885.

1.3. THE STIRRING MACHINE

As interest in rotating fluids heated up, kitchen experimentalists inevitably began to carefully observe their soup pots, coffee cups, and martini glasses, while vigorously stirring with a spoon or swizzle stick. Eventually, the professionals created a super-sophisticated version, *Couette's stirring machine,* capable of reproducible phenomena [14]. And among these phenomena were found a host of reliable examples of the bifurcation effects discovered by Poincaré among his analytical formulas:

Stellar evolution had come to earth!

1.3.1. One way to stir water in a glass (not necessarily the best) is with a rotating cylindrical rod. Although inefficient at the cocktail bar, great progress has been made in experimental fluid dynamics this way. Since its earliest days a century ago, this experiment of Mallock and Couette has been repeated over and over, with ever improving rods, cylinders, motors, and observing methods. As the speed of rotation is gradually increased, an experimental comment on the problem of Tchebychev is reliably obtained.

Although the shape of the outer envelope of the fluid is constrained by the glass and the rod, the inner structure is seen to depart very quickly from a homogeneous form (layered rotating cylinders) to a highly structured form of nonuniform motion. We show this inner structure in three representations:

(a) the fluid seen from the outside

(b) the velocity vectorfield within the fluid

(c) as a point in the state space

First, we begin with a still fluid and no rotation.

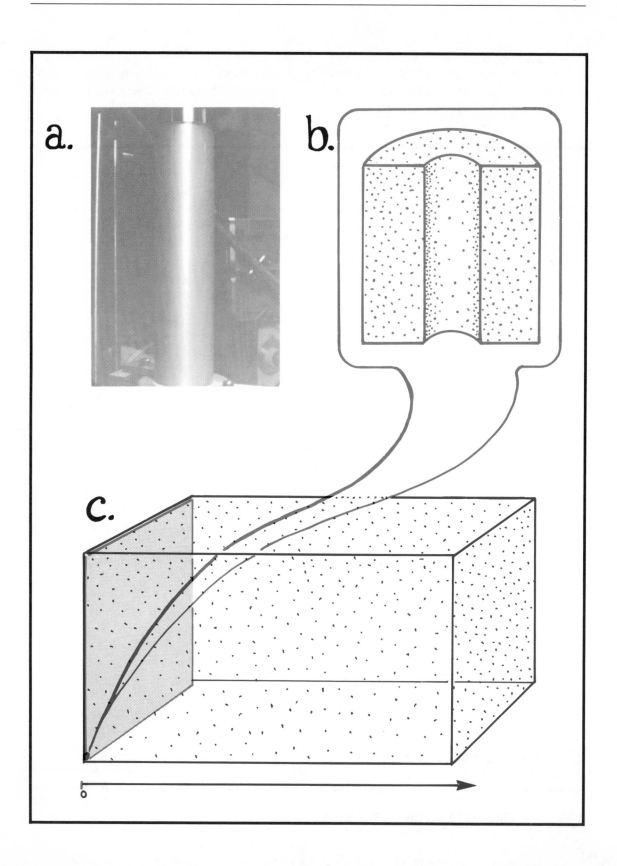

1.3.2. a. Through the side of the outer cylinder, we see a homogeneous fluid mass at rest. The fluid fills a three dimensional space in the shape of a thick tube, which we will call the *fluid domain.* (We are grateful to Rob Shaw and Russ Donnelly for these photos of an actual Couette machine).

1.3.2. b. One mathematical model for the state of the fluid is the *velocity vectorfield* in the fluid domain (here shaded in red). At each point in this domain is drawn a vector representing the velocity of the particle of the fluid passing through the selected point at the instant of observation. As in this first instance the fluid is at rest, the velocity vectors are all zero. They are shown as red dots in this illustration.

1.3.2. c. The entire velocity vectorfield may be regarded as a mathematical point in a huge (infinite dimensional) space of all possible velocity vector fields, the *state space.* And since the velocity vector at each point in the cylinder of fluid is zero, this point in the state space of all vector fields is zero as well. Thus, it is located at the *origin* (or zero vector) of the infinite dimensional state space. Here we show the state space as a vertical plane (in schematic rather than pictorial representation) outlined in green. The observed state of the fluid, represented here by the red dot in the green plane, is actually an *attractor* of a dynamical system (infinite dimensional vectorfield) on the green state space, which will call the *superdynamic* (for example, the Navier-Stokes equations) according to fluid dynamical theory [15].

The third dimension, extending to the right, represents the *control parameter:* the speed of rotation, or equivalently, the Reynolds number. This composite picture of the state space (vertical plane) and the control parameter (horizontal line) may be called the *response space,* here shaded blue. Within it, the *response diagram* will be drawn, showing the loci of the attractors as the controls are varied.

In the response space, the zero velocity vectorfield is shown as point, the red dot, in the state space furthest to the left (outlined in green) corresponding to the zero value of the control parameter (no rotation).

Next, we gradually begin a slow rotation of the rod, and let the system relax into a state of constant stirring.

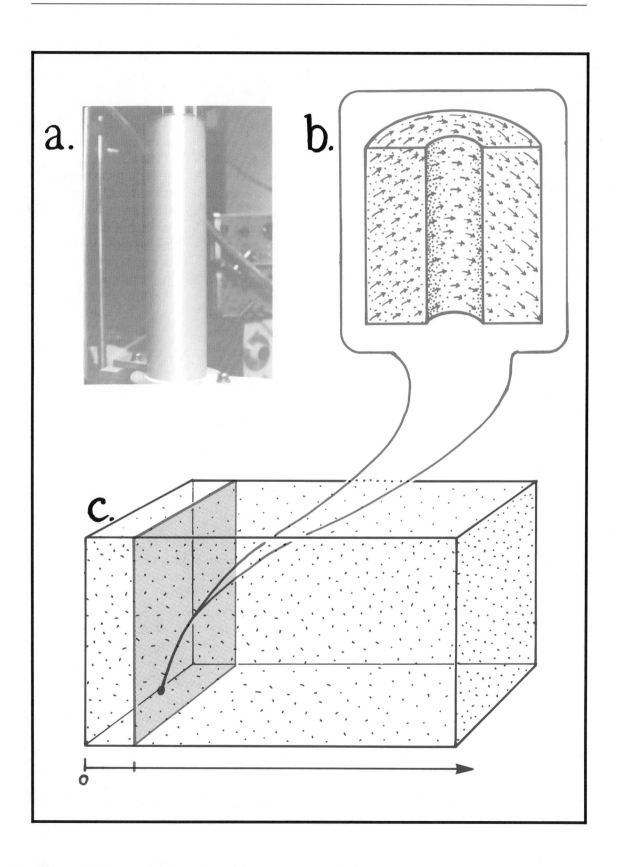

1.3.3. a. Through the side of the outer cylinder, we see a homogeneous fluid mass in uniform rotation. Each particle of fluid is moving along a horizontal circle at a constant rate. The rate is zero for the largest circles at the outer glass cylinder, it is fixed by the speed of rotation of the rod at the smallest circles, and in the interior of the fluid, it varies uniformly between these extremes.

1.3.3. b. Here is the velocity vectorfield in the fluid domain, revealed by some trajectories of fluid particles, drawn in red. It shows the circular motion of the fluid, with the smaller velocities outside, and the higher speeds inside. At any chosen point in the fluid domain, this velocity vector is at rest, it does not change with time while we are observing.

1.3.3. c. Here we view the velocity vectorfield as a single point in the response space. And since the velocity vector at each point in the fluid domain is at rest, this point in the response space is at rest as well. This red point is located within the vertical plane (state space of all velocity vectorfields) shaded in green, corresponding to a small value of the control parameter. And within that green plane, it is near the origin, indicating a small range of actual fluid velocities within the fluid domain. The black line passing through the red dot represents the track of the red dot as the control parameter is varied, and is called the *locus of attraction*. Generally, the *response diagram* ignifies the record of all the loci of attraction known for the given experimental system, drawn within this blue response space. The job of the experimentalist is to create this record.

We will now try to discover a locus of attraction for the stirring machine, by continuing to increase the speed of rotation.

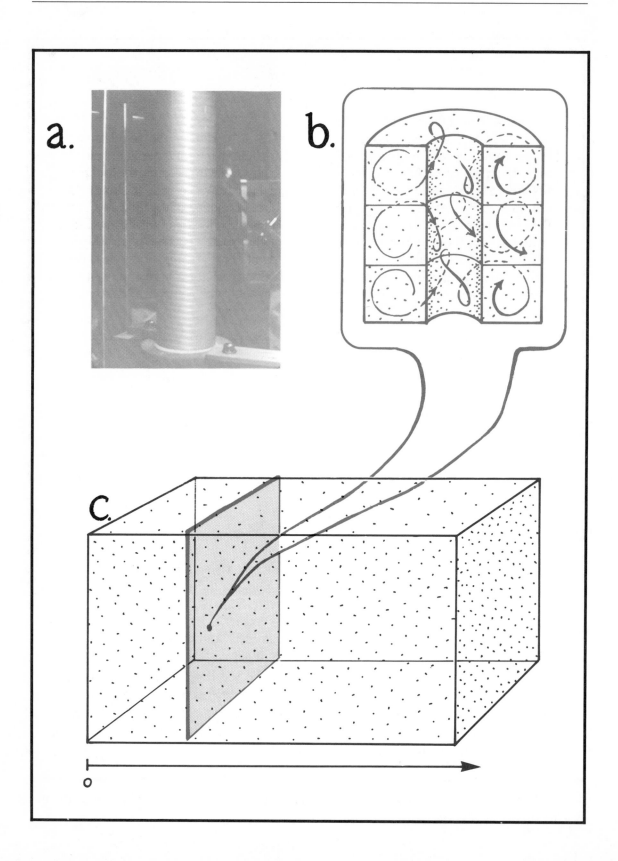

1.3.4. a. After a moderate increase in the rate of stirring, this is one mode we are likely to see through the walls of the stirring machine. The fluid motion has separated into a stack of ring-shaped cells, divided by flat boundaries evenly spaced along the axis of rotation.

The boundaries are still. These are the *Taylor cells* discovered by Taylor in 1923.

1.3.4. b. Upon closer inspection (sometimes aluminum powder is put in the fluid to show the motion more more clearly) we see that the fluid motion in each cell is *solenoidal.* One cell is a clockwise vortex, the next counter- clockwise, and so on. Here, the velocity vectorfield is indicated by some exemplary red trajectories. In spite of the increasingly complicated fluid motion, the vectorfield is still *stationary.* It is a point attractor of the superdynamic.

1.3.4. c. Here is the current situation, represented in the response diagram. The current state (velocity vectorfield) is shown as a red dot (point attractor) in the appropriate state space (shaded in green) somewhat to the right of the state space outlined in the previous sequence. Note that the locus of attraction (black curve through the red dot) has a gap just to the left of the yoke. This is due to a bifurcation event called the *static fold,* and related to the pitchfork bifurcation discovered by Jacobi in 1834 in his study of the figure of the Earth. The observation of this event requires careful experimental work, repeatedly turning the speed control up and down.

Now we make an substantial increase in the rate of the stirring rod, to see what turns up.

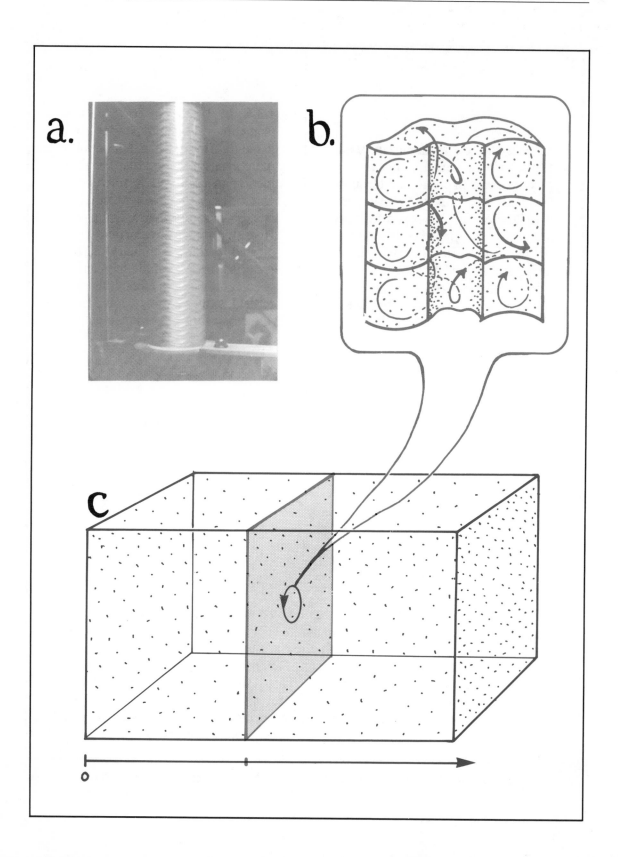

1.3.5. a. We now see, looking directly at the fluid through the side of the outer cylinder, that the Taylor cell boundaries have developed waves, and the wavy cells are slowly rotating around the central axis [16].

1.3.5. b. This *wavy vortex* phenomenon is represented by a velocity vectorfield in the fluid domain, shown here in stop motion drawing, which is slowly (and periodically) varying in time. The pattern shown here repeats every few seconds.

1.3.5. c. Representing this stop motion vectorfield as a red dot in the state space (here outlined in green as usual) and waiting a few seconds, we would see it move around a small cycle. The periodic change in the fluid velocity vectorfield indicates that we are observing a *periodic attractor* of the superdynamic. And the black locus of attraction, to the left of this red cycle, shows a change from a static to a periodic attractor. This exhibits yet another bifurcation, discovered by Poincaré in 1885 and successfully analysed by Hopf in 1942. This event will be described in further detail later in this volume.

Now we make a further increase in the rate of rotation of the stirring rod, and discover chaos!

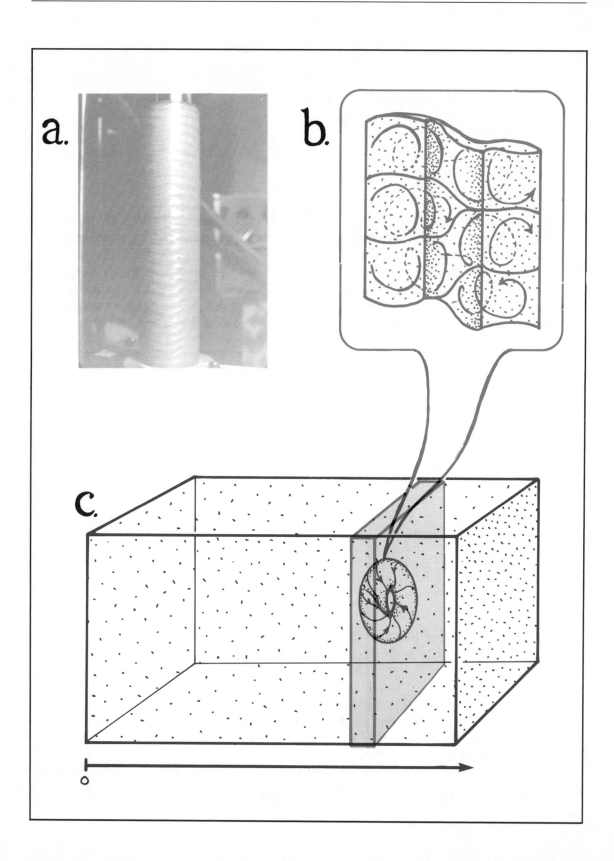

a.

b.

c.

o

1.3.6. a. After things settle down as much as they ever will, we may see that some rings are pinched off. The complete rings are still wavy vortices, but they wave irregularly. Worse still, the pinched cells may jump around. This is mild turbulence!

1.3.6. b. The velocity vectorfield, at a single instant of observation, is very complicated, but still understandable. Over time, however, it wanders erratically about, and never returns to an exact copy of an earlier state.

1.3.6. c. The wandering of the red dot within the green state space (shown here as a three-dimensional box, to give us adequate space in which to represent its shape) fills out with a thickened torus, perhaps, or some other *chaotic attractor* (see *Part Two* of this series) of the superdynamic. The black locus of attraction has suffered some further bifurcation, the *onset of chaos*. Its entire history, from the far left to this point, is called a *chaotic scenario*.

Finally, we thrust the speed control to the maximum.

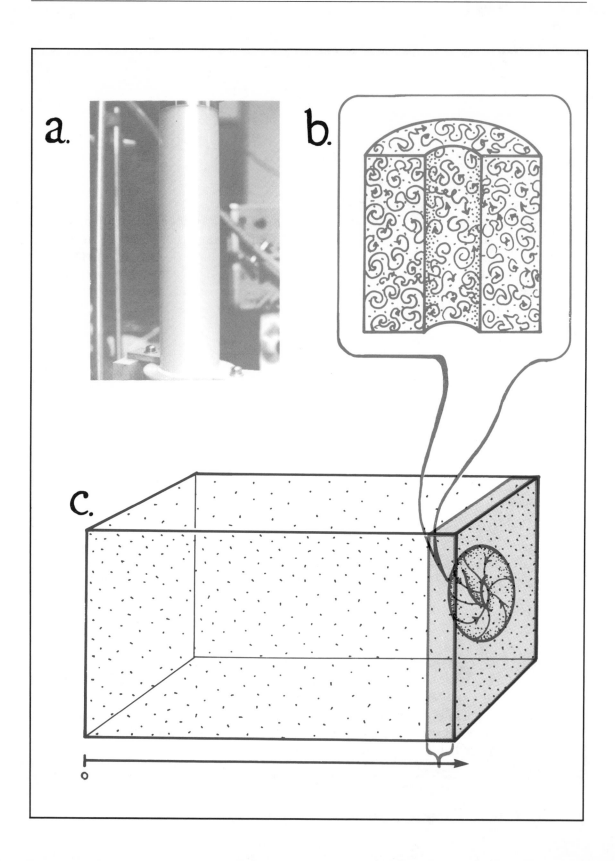

1.3.7. a. Hang on to your kayak, there is white water everywhere!

1.3.7. b. The velocity vectorfield, drawn here in stop motion, is beyond understanding.

1.3.7. c. The motion of the red dot within the green state space, again traced over a few seconds, describes a chaotic attractor of the superdynamic as before. Here the attractor is shown as a bagel (*Part Two,* Section 3.2) although in reality it might be much more complicated. This is fully developed turbulence! The black locus of attraction has suffered further bifurcations, from one type of chaos to another, which are little understood at present.

1.4 THE BIG PICTURE

In the first two sections of this historical introduction to the concepts of bifurcation theory, we kept our feet on the ground. We spoke about physical phenomena and their simplest mathematical models. In the third section we introduced a four-fold visual representation:

1. the physical phenomena,

2. their simplest mathematical representation (velocity vectorfield in fluid domain, stop-motion or time-varying),

3. more abstract mathematical representation (red dot moving upon red attractor in green state space),

4. green state space moving within blue response diagram, while red attractor drags along black locus of attraction.

We now wish to take one last leap, to a bigger picture of bifurcation theory, introduced by René Thom in his revolutionary text of 1972 [17] on structural stability.

We will again use the Couette machine as an example, but the rotating blob or the game of bob (see *Part One*) would do as well. What we must keep in mind in these examples is that the fundamental model is not a dynamical system, such as the superdynamic of fluid mechanics. Instead, the central object of bifurcation theory is a *dynamical scheme,* that is, a dynamical system *depending upon control parameters.* For example, in the dynamical model for the Couette machine, the *superdynamic depends on the stirring speed.* Thus also, the phase portrait of the dynamical system depends on the controls, and putting these pictures side-by-side generates the response diagram.

We are now going to leap to the ultimate abstraction: the superspace of all superdynamics.

In the preceding section we imploded an instantaneous state of a complex physical system and regarded it as simply a single point of a geometrical model, the state space. The dynamical model for the evolution of these instantaneous states in time consists of a dynamical system, which we have been calling the superdynamic in this context. In general, it is just called the dynamic, or the dynamical rule, etc. This representation assumes that the control parameter is fixed at a constant value.

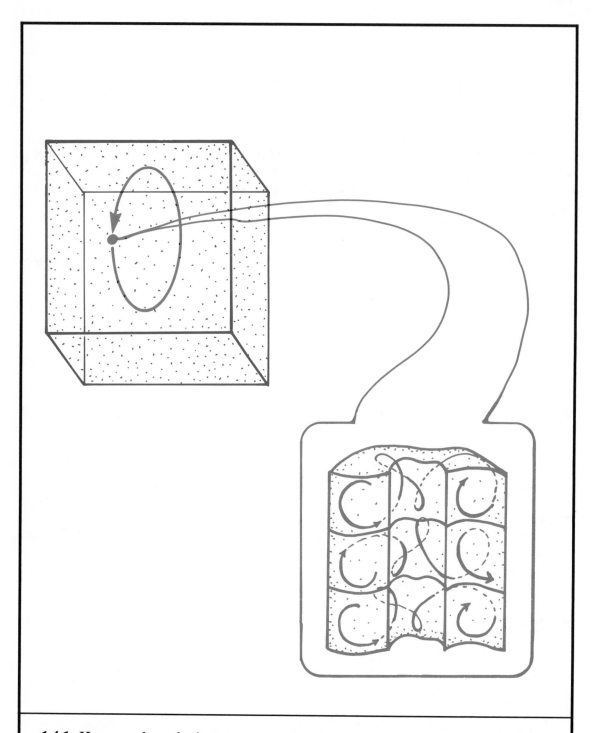

1.4.1. Here we show the instantaneous state scrunched to a single red point of the state space, on which the dynamic is indicated by the blue curves. The red cycle denotes a periodic attractor, such as that observed in Figure 1.3.5.

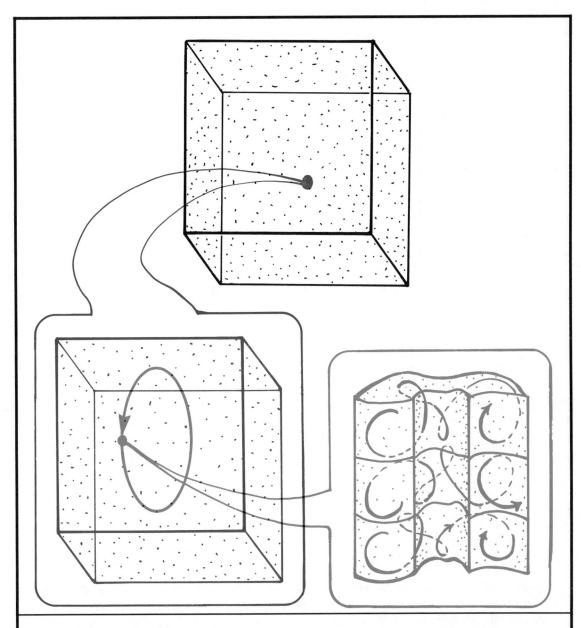

1.4.2. Here we have scrunched once again, so that the superdynamic becomes represented by a single point in *dynamical superspace*, Thom's Big Picture, within which every superdynamic on the given state space is represented by a single point. Every state space has its own personal superspace.

We now use superspace to construct an alternative to the response diagram as a representation of a dynamical scheme, or dynamical system depending on control parameters. We start with a small piece of the response diagram developed in the preceding section, in Fig. 1.3.5.

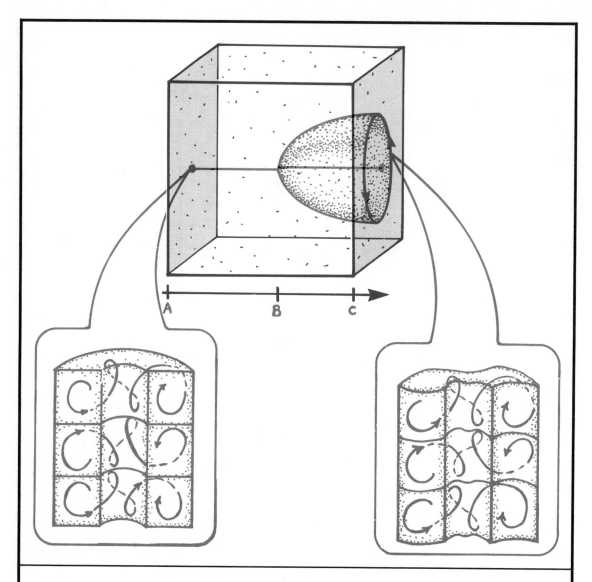

1.4.3. Here the control parameter increases a small amount from A to C, the cylinder of fluid changes from flat vortices (point attractor) to wavy vortices (periodic attractor) as the control passes B, and the locus of attraction has the form of a goblet. This is an example of a bifurcation event called *excitation,* also known as the *Hopf bifurcation.* It is treated in more detail in the next section.

We now transform this picture into superspace. Each and every value of the control parameter specifies a copy of the state space having its own superdynamic. That is, the control parameter changes the dynamical rule but not the state space. In this scrunch, each of these super-dynamics becomes a single point in superspace. We may think of this scrunch as a move-ment of the control space (the blue interval in the preceding panel) into superspace. The result is the blue curve in this picture of superspace.

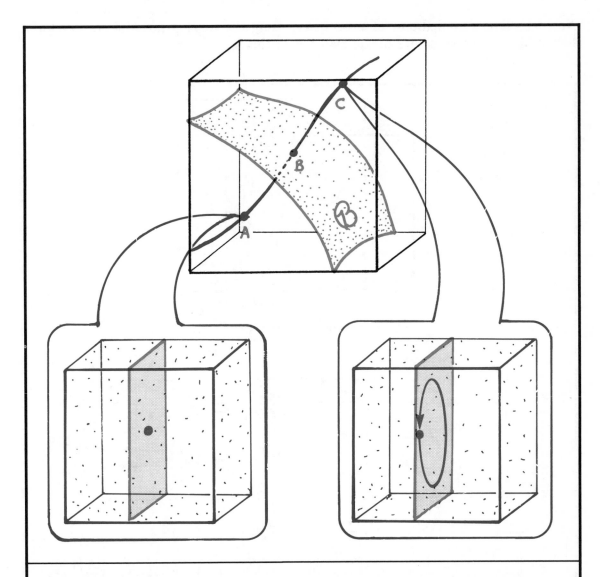

1.4.4. See that the starting superdynamic determined by A corresponds to the lower endpoint of this curve, the final superdynamic determined by C corresponds to the upper endpoint of this curve, and the bifurcation point B corresponds to an intermediate point in the curve, shown here at the intersection of the blue curve and a red surface. This red surface is part of the *Bad Set*.

As Andronov discovered in 1937, the bad set consists of dynamical systems which are *not structurally stable* (see Ch. 3 of *Part Three* of this series for the definition). One of the numerous contributions of René Thom to dynamical systems theory is a Big Picture of the bad set within superspace, a strategy for analysing its structure, and a recognition of this structure as a kind of universal Platonic model for morphogenetic (evolutionary) processes in Nature.

Now let's take a guided tour of superspace, using the stirring machine, to develop a better idea of the structure of the Bad Set in the Big Picture.

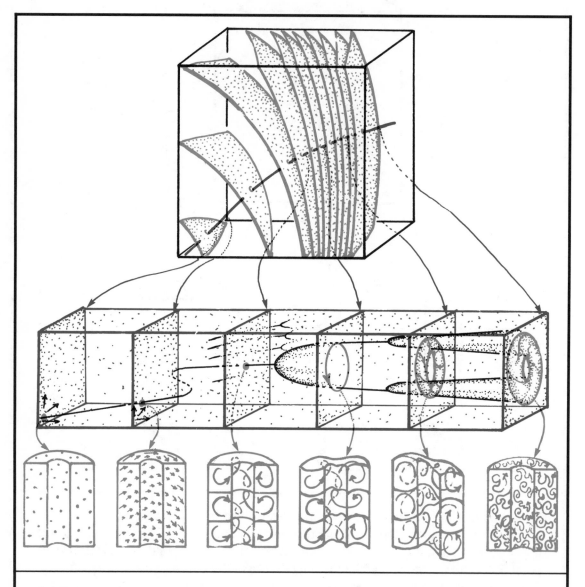

1.4.5. Here is the entire response diagram developed in the preceding section, all scrunched onto a curve in the Big Picture. Each and every bifurcation located in the preceding discussion identifies a sheet of the Bad Set. There are infinitely many of these sheets, which accumulate in Fat Fractals, as we shall see later in this book.

The balance of this work is a pictorial atlas of bifurcations which are generic for dynamical schemes depending upon a single control parameter. They identify only the largest structures of the Bad Set.

2. SUBTLE BIFURCATIONS

The early history of the bifurcation idea unrolled in the context of physical systems demanding infinite dimensional dynamical models, based upon partial differential equations. In the revolutionary work of Poincaré, the connection was made with dynamical systems of finite dimension, based upon ordinary differential equations. The recent history of bifurcation theory has therefore been developed along two parallel tracks. In the sequel of this work, we concentrate on the finite dimensional case, *dynamical bifurcation theory (DBT)*. The parallel theory for systems of partial differential equations, which we occasionally call *classical bifurcation theory (CBT)*, may be developed in a similar fashion. Unfortunately, we will not be able to indicate the fantastic importance of this theory in applications. Our view, often expressed in other writings, is that the response diagrams of these atomic bifurcation events comprise our most important source of models for the dynamical processes of nature. For some support of this view, see the seminal works of Thom [1] and Prigogine [2]. Thus, this final volume of this series, *Part Four,* is the culmination and main motive for the entire work of four years (comprising four volumes, 800 pages, and 800 illustrations). The bifurcations of DBT may be classified in three types: *subtle bifurcations, catastrophic bifurcations (catastrophes),* and *explosive bifurcations (explosions).*

In this Chapter, we present the subtle bifurcations in their simplest versions.

2.1. FIRST EXCITATION

We have already encountered the first excitation, known to Poincaré in 1885 and analyzed by Hopf in 1942, as the second event in the bifurcation sequence of the stirring machine, (see Fig. 1.3.5). It is most frequently called the *Hopf bifurcation.* There are at least two complete texts on this phenomenon alone. One of these [3] contains a section on the recent history and numerous applications of the event. The other [4] develops very early applications to the speed governor (for the steam engine invented by Watt in 1782) ascribed to Airy (1840), Maxwell (1868) and Vyshnegradskii (1876). Both have very detailed analyses and extensive bibliographies, and are highly reccommended.

We will describe simple excitation in the context of radio transmitters developed in *Part One,* Sections 3.3 and 5.6, and in *Part Two,* Section 3.2.

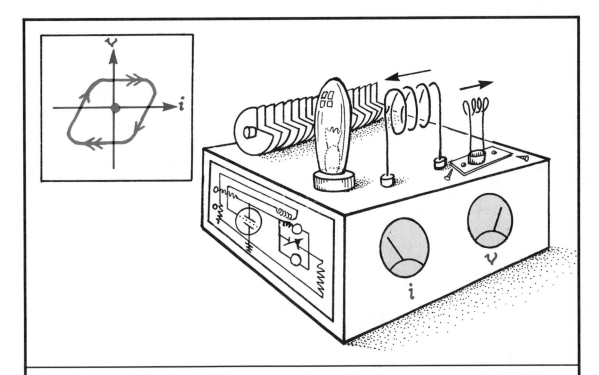

2.1.1. Here is the antique transmitter, as used by Marconi and Van der Pol. We have specially prepared it for this experiment by loosening the screws at the base of the small feedback coil, so that it may be easily rotated a half turn or so in either direction. In this figure, the coil is in the normal position, the current and voltage in the larger tank coil are oscillating, and the transmitter is ''on the air.'' A plot of the current and voltage (shown in the window) is tracking a periodic attractor clockwise.

In this exercise, the small coil will be our control knob.

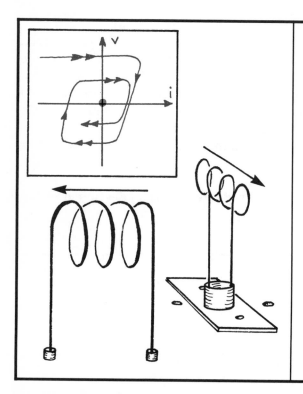

2.1.2. Now we grab the small coil from above and twist it more than a quarter turn to the right. If not electrocuted, we find that the transmitter quits, the oscillations gradually die out, and the plotted measurements follow an exponential spiral down to the point attractor at the origin of the state space. We are off the air!

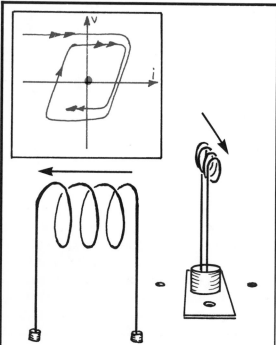

2.1.3. Grabbing the small coil again, we slowly untwist it a few degrees, trying to undo the damage. No change in the situation, so we keep on untwisting.

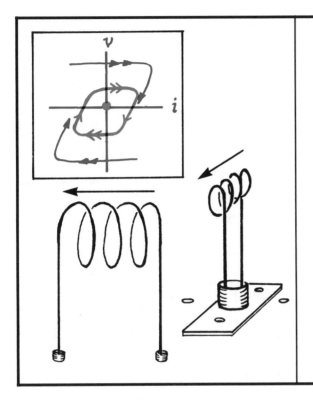

2.1.4. After we pass a quarter turn by a few degrees, the oscillations resume, but very feebly! The phase portrait (window) shows a very small periodic attractor encircling a point repellor at the origin.

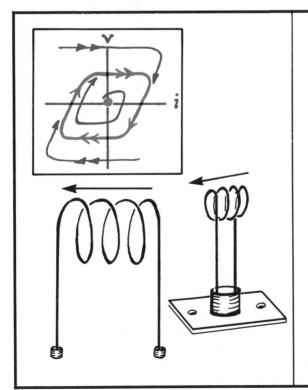

2.1.5. Now slowly untwist the coil some more, gradually returning to the original position. The oscillation grows stronger, and the audience may hear a feeble broadcast, which grows stronger and becomes normal.

This is a *subtle* bifurcation, as the qualitative change in the behavior of the transmitter is almost imperceptible. The small coil orientation is the control parameter, and for each orientation there is a different dynamical system modeling the transmitter, according to Van der Pol. (The parameter is represented by B in Example 4a of the Appendix of *Part One*. The other parameters are fixed.) We now put together, side by side, the phase portraits shown in the window of the last few panels. To relate the phenomenon to the qualitative theory of rest points, we will add to each portrait the CEs of the critical point of the origin (see Section 1.4 of *Part Two)*.

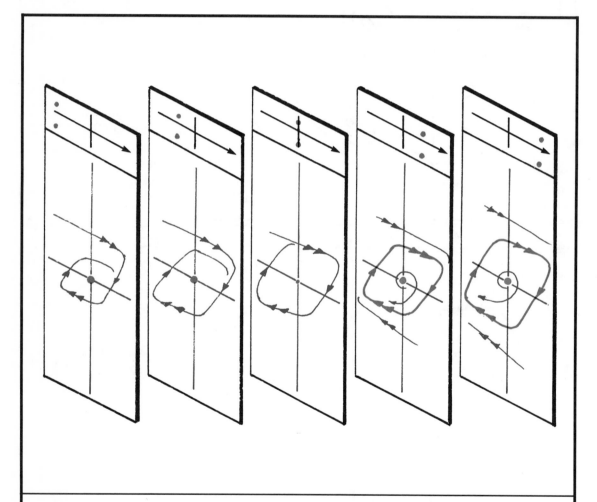

2.1.6. Arranging the phase portraits in order, we obtain this record of behavior, with the CEs shown in the windows. They may be obtained from the equations defining the scheme, by means of algorithms given in texts of linear algebra [5]. Here we have added, at the moment of bifurcation, an additional phase portrait. This portrait, shown as a *center* (concentric periodic trajectories), is generally a very weak spiral in or out. But it will look like a center to the casual observer.

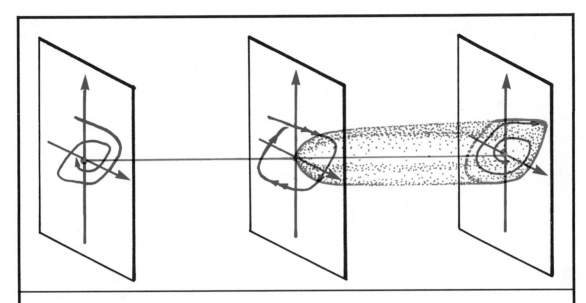

2.1.7. We now erect these portraits and arrange them in their proper places within the response diagram of Van der Pol's dynamical scheme. We call this display a *side-by-side* representation. It is a sort of skeleton of the full response diagram.

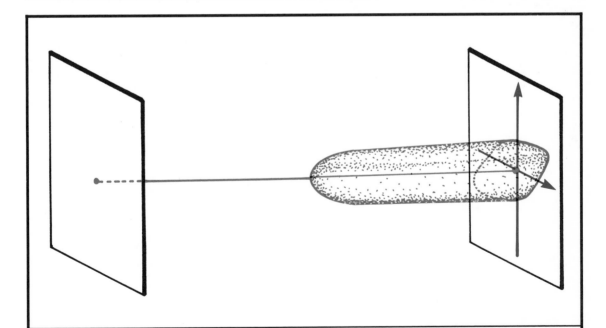

2.1.8. Finally we strip away the technical detail, and connect up the skeletons to form this mnemonic version of the response diagram, called the *cut-away* representation, suitable for framing. The joint of the goblet, where the stem joins the cup, is the bifurcation event. Near it, the goblet has a smooth parabolic shape.

SUMMARY. In the first excitation, a point attractor of spiral type gradually weakens (its complex CEs move toward the right, approaching the imaginary axis) and destabilizes (the CEs cross to right half-plane) while emitting a periodic attractor. The period of oscillation of the new attractor is determined by the CEs of the origin, at the moment of its creation. The amplitude of the new attractor grows gradually as the control parameter continues to increase, creating the parabolic goblet shape shown in Fig. 2.1.8.

The *bifurcation point* (the critical value of the control parameter at which the CEs cross the imaginary axis) is a quarter turn of the coil in this case. At the bifurcation point, the critical point at the origin is not elementary, it is a center (see *Part Three,* Section 2.1). Thus, by Peixoto's theorem, the dynamical system corresponding to this bifurcation point is not structurally stable (see *Part Three,* Section 3.2). The arc in the Big Picture described by this dynamical scheme (see Fig. 1.3.4 above) pierces the bad set at the bifurcation point only.

The locus of this new periodic attractor *branches off* from the locus of the critical point. We may say that *stability is lost* by the critical point at the origin, and passes to the limit cycle. This event is also described as the *excitation of a mode of oscillation,* a mode which (before excitation) is implicit in the point attractor of spiral type. Such an attractor may be viewed as an attractive oscillator of amplitude zero. More details may be found in the literature, which includes entire volumes devoted entirely to this event. [3,4]

2.2. SECOND EXCITATION

The kind of excitation which we have just described can happen to an oscillator as well as to a static attractor. This event has been known since Poincaré at least, but is usually attributed to Neimark in 1959. Sometimes it is called the *secondary Hopf bifurcation*. It occurs in the bifurcation sequence of the stirring machine, but we omitted it in our description for economy.

We will now need all we have learned about the art of toral arrangement from the preceding volumes of this Series.

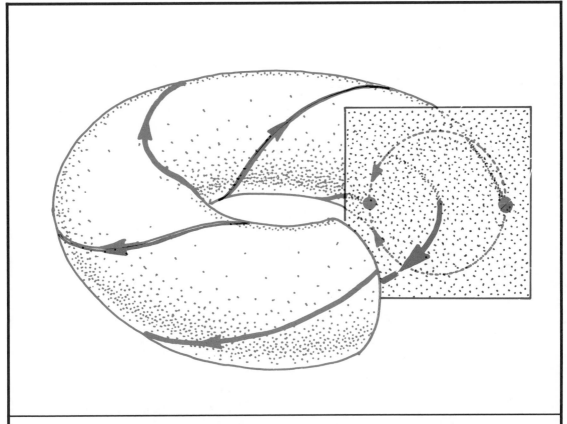

2.2.1. Recall this attractive invariant torus (AIT) from the discussion of forced oscillators in *Part One,* Section 5.3. We will now explode an innocent periodic attractor of spiral type in 3D (see *Part Two,* Section 2.5) into one of these gems.

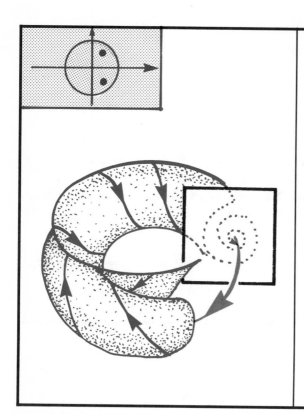

2.2.2. BEFORE: here is your garden variety spiral cycle in 3D (red for attractors) with a piece of the asymptotically attracted trajectory foliage (blue) cut away to reveal a 2D section (strobe plane, see *Part One,* 4.1). And in the window, the CMs within the unit circle, indicating the strength of attraction *(Part Two,* 2.5).

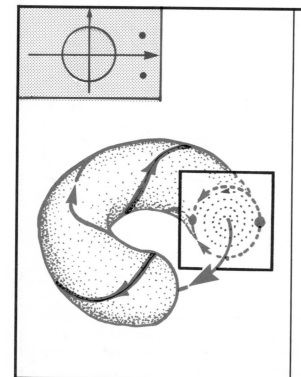

2.2.3. AFTER: The cycle has turned green, indicating repulsion, while an enclosing AIT has appeared, red indicating attraction. It is attractive, yet not necessarily an attractor. (It contains attractors, like the red curve spiraling it.) Again, the window shows the CMs of the central cycle, now outside the unit circle, showing the strength of repulsion.

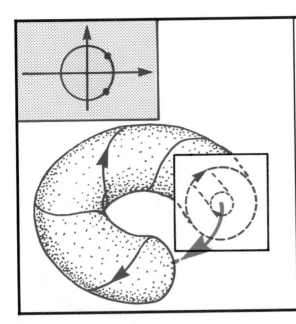

2.2.4. DURING: The bifurcation occurs as the CMs pass through the unit circle. At this moment, the central limit cycle is neither attracting nor repelling. In fact, the 2D strobe plane is filled with spirals (in or out) which are wound so tightly that they may appear to be nested invariant circles. These tight spirals correspond to scrolled insets or outsets which may appear to be nested invariant tori in the 3D flow.

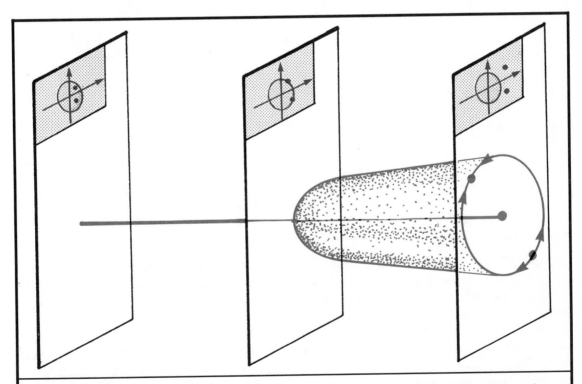

2.2.5. To construct the response diagram of this scheme, we will extract the strobe planes, and erect them side-by-side in our usual fashion. Note that it looks like the response diagram for first excitation at the end of the preceding section. But here, we are stacking strobe planes, rather than state spaces.

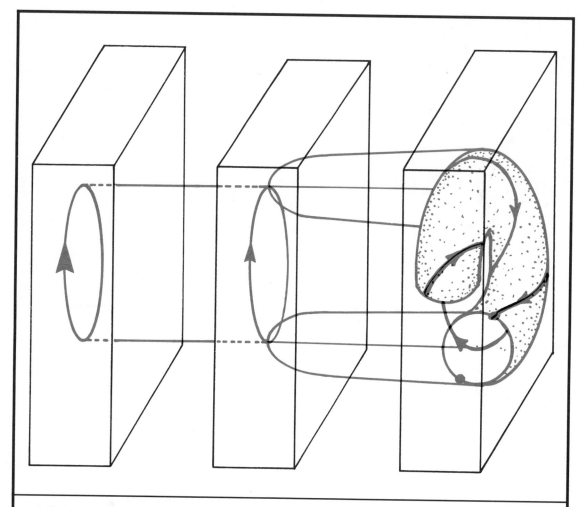

2.2.6. Finally, here is the cut-away view of the response diagram. We have abandoned the strobe planes, and replaced each with a full 3D state space, seen in 2D perspective view.

SUMMARY. In the first excitation, stability is lost by a critical point, and its implicit oscillator emerges from hiding. This event is characterized by the CEs of the critical point. But a critical point in 2D is rather like a limit cycle in 3D, as the Poincaré section (strobe plane) technique shows. And in this way a point attractor of spiral type in the plane (see *Part Two,* 1.4) corresponds to a periodic attractor in 3D of spiral type (see *Part Two,* 2.5). And the two complex conjugate CEs of the spiral point in 2D correspond to the two CMs of the spiral cycle in 3D. So by analogy, we may see in such an oscillation in 3D an infinitesimally thin torus, hiding and ready to jump out, should the attraction of the oscillator weaken. When this torus jumps out, it represents a *compound oscillation of two modes,* such as we have studied in the context of two coupled oscillators in *Part One,* Ch. 5. If the original oscillator is considered the first mode, then the new torus may be regarded as the combination of the original mode with a new, second mode. Hence the name, *second excitation.*

2.3. OCTAVE JUMP IN 2D

The main feature of this event is the replacement of a periodic attractor by another one of twice the period. If this happened while a musical instrument was holding a note and some parameter was being adjusted, you would hear a very soft tone begin an octave below, and gradually increase in volume.

Here are some computer plots of actual simulations of an octave jump in a 3D system, provided by Rob Shaw.

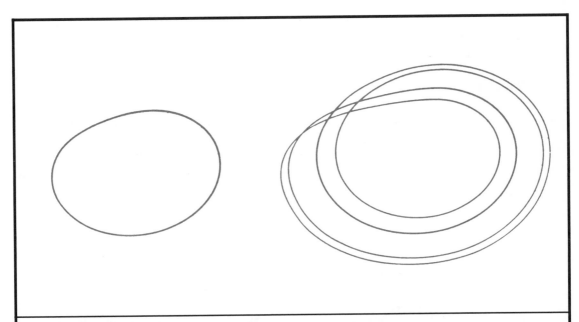

2.3.1. BEFORE: Trajectory tracing around a periodic attractor in the 3D state space, but projected into the 2D screen of the oscilloscope.

AFTER: Trajectory tracing around a different periodic attractor. Note that this one follows closely the track of the previous one. But after one revolution, it does not quite close. After a second circuit, it closes upon itself exactly. Note that the trajectory does not cross itself, as that is highly illegal for dynamical systems. But it appears to, because of the projection onto the 2D viewing screen.

Now we will replot these trajectories in an intrinsically 2D context. A Möbius band is necessary to accommodate the negative real CM, as explained in *Part Two, 2.2.*

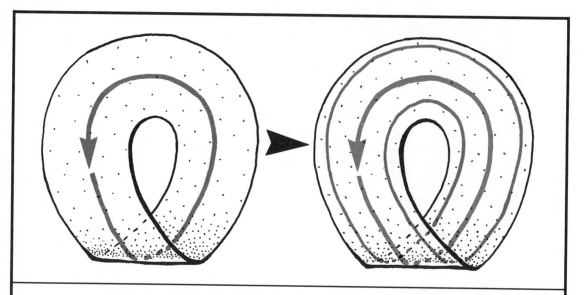

2.3.2. BEFORE: We start with a dynamical system on the band having a single periodic attractor (red) which goes once around.

AFTER: This new system has a single periodic attractor which goes twice around the band, without crossing itself. The former attractor still exists as a repellor (green).

Here is a review of the CMs of the central cycle, from *Part Two*, 2.2.

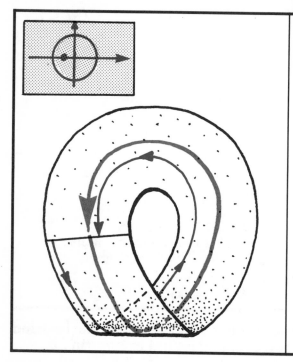

2.3.3. BEFORE: Draw a strobe line (black) across the band. The negative real CM means that a nearby trajectory (blue) starting on the strobe line to the left of the red cycle will return to the right (and closer) after one circuit. Thus, the strobe line is reversed by the first-return map, and the inset must be twisted.

The CM is shown in the window. While negative, it is within the unit circle (blue), signifying attraction.

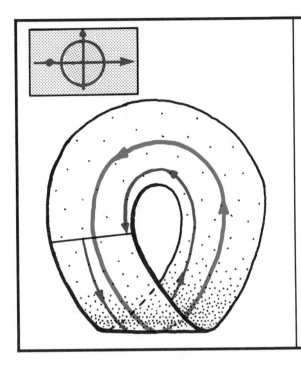

2.3.4. AFTER: Again draw a strobe line across the band. The CM is still negative. A nearby trajectory starting on the strobe line to the left of the green cycle will still return to the right (but further away) after one circuit.

The CM is again shown in the window. While negative, it is outside the unit circle, signifying repulsion. The cycle is drawn in green, as it is repulsive.

Between these two portraits there is a bifurcation.

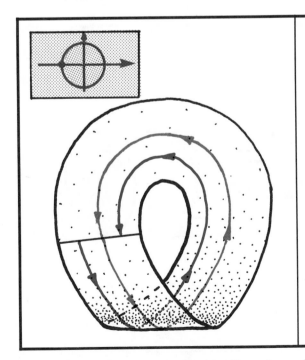

2.3.5. DURING: The CM, still negative, is actually sitting at minus one on the negative real axis. A nearby trajectory starting on the strobe line to the left of the red cycle will still return to the right (but at the same distance from the red cycle) after one circuit.

The CM is again shown in the window. While negative, it is on the unit circle, signifying neither attraction nor repulsion. This situation is structurally unstable, according to Peixoto's theorem (see *Part Three*, 3.2).

We now put these portraits together, in a side-by-side representation of the response diagram.

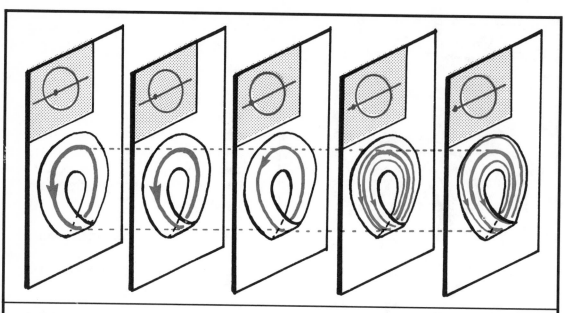

2.3.6. Reading from left to right, the red cycle turns green at the instant of bifurcation. A new red cycle branches off gradually, but it must go twice around to close on itself. Note that the CM of the new periodic attractor is positive, and within the unit circle.

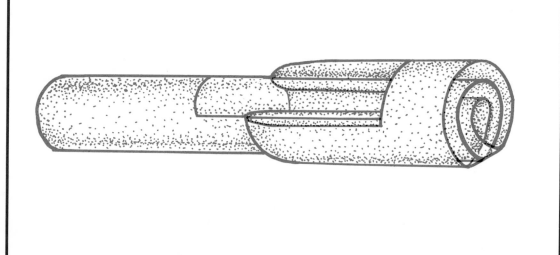

2.3.7. And finally, a cut-away representation, for the collection.

SUMMARY: A periodic attractor on a Möbius band responds to a control parameter by losing stability. Its CM journeys outward, seeking to escape. Upon the CM crossing the unit circle, this limit cycle becomes a repellor, and a new periodic attractor is born. This has twice the period, hence half the frequency. Its fundamental is one octave down. However, it traces closely around the same track twice before closing, so its second harmonic (same tone as the recently vanished attractor) is strong. Thus, this bifurcation event is subtle, in that its detection is possible only after the new behavior grows strong. One cannot detect the exact moment of bifurcation by casual observation. This is in marked contrast to the explosive and catastrophic events, as we shall soon see. Some people like to call this event a *period doubling bifurcation*.

2.4. OCTAVE JUMP IN 3D

Of course the octave jump can happen in 3D, 4D, and so on. In this section we illustrate one of several scenarios in 3D.

We begin with a periodic attractor of nodal type.

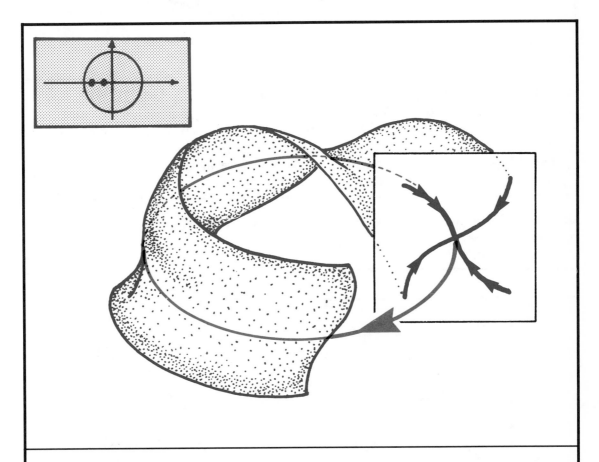

2.4.1. BEFORE: Recall this nodal saddle in 3D from *Part Two,* Fig. 2.4.3. Note that both of its CMs are negative reals within the unit circle. Its inset, a solid 3D ring, contains two invariant surfaces, both Möbius bands (blue). One of these, the *fast band,* corresponds to the smaller CM (closer to the origin). Trajectories on this band spiral toward the red attractor faster than the others. The other, the *slow band,* corresponds to the other CM (for slow traffic only).

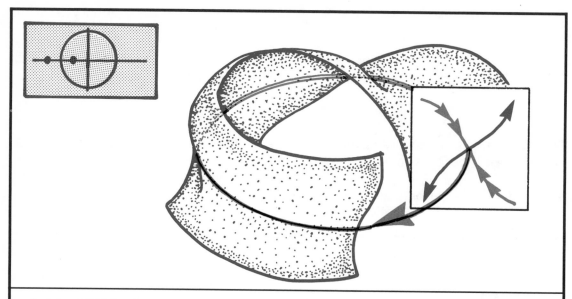

2.4.2. AFTER: Here is another old acquaintance, a saddle cycle in 3D from *Part Two,* Figure 2.3.10. Both CMs are negative real, but only one is within the unit circle. It corresponds to a twisted band as before, but now this band is the entire inset. The other CM is outside the unit circle, and corresponds to the outset, another twisted band. These two bands are oriented exactly like those in the BEFORE panel, but now one of them is the outset, rather than the slow band.

But this AFTER portrait has an additional feature, which we shall reveal with strobe sections.

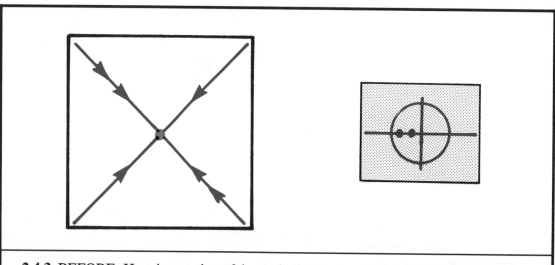

2.4.3. BEFORE: Here is a section of the periodic attractor (red) of nodal type, showing the section curves (green) of the fast and slow bands within its inset, and the CMs.

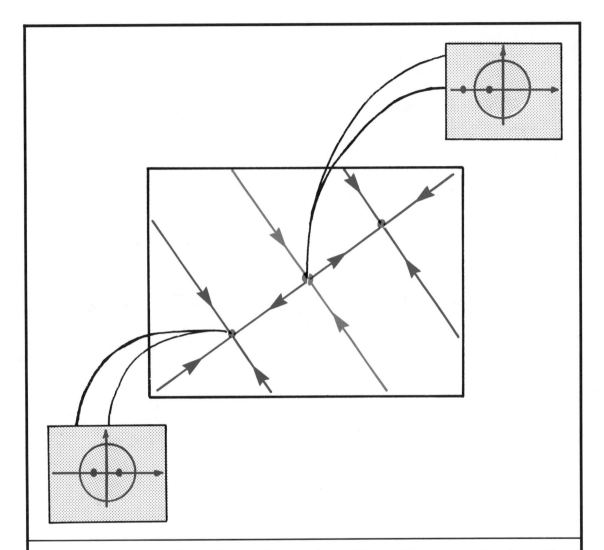

2.4.4. AFTER: And here likewise is a section of the saddle cycle (red and green) with its inset (green) and outset (blue). But here we have added an additional feature to the sectional portrait. Notice the two red dots. These are two successive passages of the same trajectory, a periodic attractor, through the strobe plane. The CMs of the new attractor are shown in the window on the left.

To understand this 3D phase portrait, just take the AFTER portrait of Fig. 2.3.2, and imbed it here as the outset of the saddle. This octave jump in 3D is identical to the 2D event on a Möbius band, but taking place entirely on this fixed band through our central cycle. The attraction along the fast inset does not change during this event. This 3D bifurcation is an extension of the preceding 2D bifurcation.

Here is the view of the response diagram made from erecting the strobe planes side-by-side.

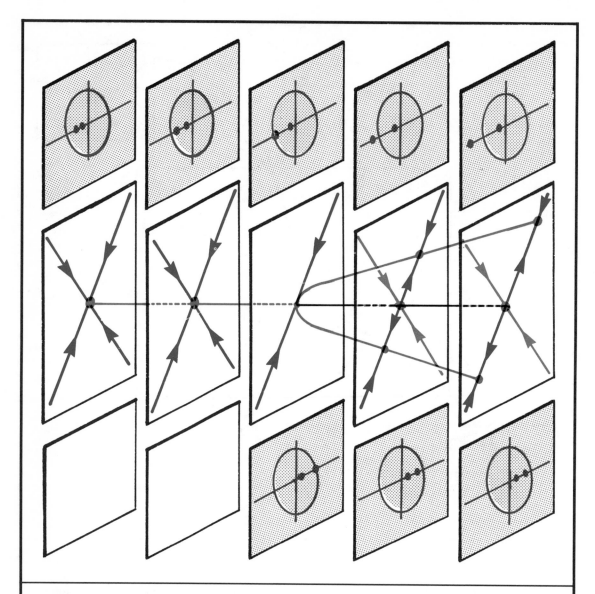

2.4.5. From left to right, the strength of attraction of the slow band of the nodal attractor progressively weakens (outer CM moves further out) and turns to repulsion at the bifurcation point (as the outer CM transits the unit circle). The speed of attraction of the fast band (inner CM) is unaffected by the control parameter. The progress of the CMs of the original cycle are shown in the upper window.

A new attractor is subtly born, which closes only after two circuits of the 3D ring. This is shown, after the event, as two disjoint red points. They spread roughly parabolically as the control parameter continues to increase. The CMs of the new attractor are roughly the square of those of the original cycle. These are shown in the lower window.

SUMMARY: This event is not a new entry in our encyclopedia of generic bifurcation diagrams for single control schemes. It is just the extension to 3D of the preceding entry, the octave jump in 2D, to suggest the variety of possible presentations of a single universal form in the Big Picture.

3. FOLD CATASTROPHES

As explained earlier, there are three kinds of bifurcations with one control in DBT: subtle, catastrophic, and explosive. The previous chapter surveyed the simplest occurences of the best known subtle bifurcations, and there are not many known bifurcations in this class. But catastrophic bifurcations are very numerous, and this chapter and the following two will be devoted to them. The chief feature of a catastrophe is the disappearance of an attractor, along with its entire basin. This can occur to any type of attractor — whether static, periodic, or chaotic — in a variety of ways. The catastrophic bifurcations of static attractors comprise the subject matter of *elementary catastrophe theory (ECT)* [1].

In this chapter, we introduce the simplest one: pairwise annihilation, also called the *fold catastrophe.*

3.1. STATIC FOLD IN 1D

A favorite way for an attractor to disappear, as the control parameter of a dynamical scheme is varied, is like the moth and the flame. The attractor drifts slowly towards the separatrix at the edge of its basin. When it arrives, three things disappear simultaneously: the attractor, its basin, and its separatrix. In this section we illustrate the simplest case of this type of catastrophe: the ID (one-dimensional) case.

We will make use of the CE of the critical point of a dynamical system in 1D.

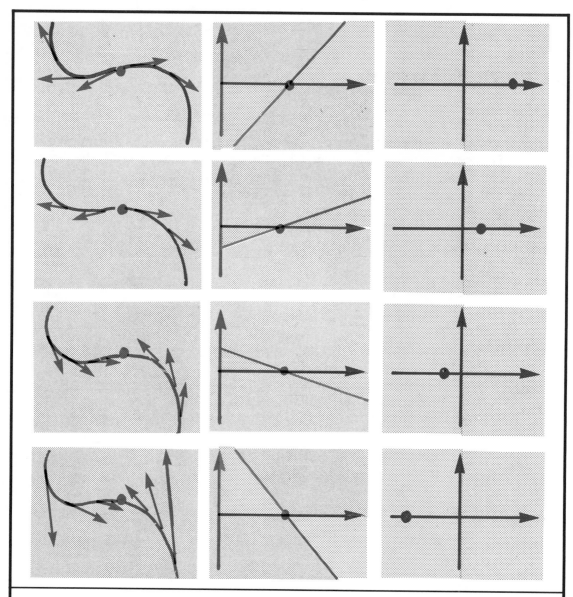

3.1.1. Recall this tabulation of the hyperbolic critical points in 1D from *Part Two,* Fig. 1.1.8. Here we introduce our predominant color code: attractors are red (all trajectories *stop)* and repellors are *green* (all trajectories *go).* At the same time, insets are green *(gr-in)* and outsets are blue *(bl-out).* Meanwhile, the velocity vectors in the first column are red (a temporary expedient) and the inclined red lines in the middle column are the graphs of the vectorfield as a function of position in the (horizontal) state space. The right column indicates the position of the CE (blue) in the CE plane of complex numbers. The CE (blue point) in the green region indicates repulsion. The one in the red region indicates attraction. See *Part Two* for more explanation of the CEs.

Having recalled this technical background from *Part Two,* we are now ready for our first fold catastrophe: the static fold.

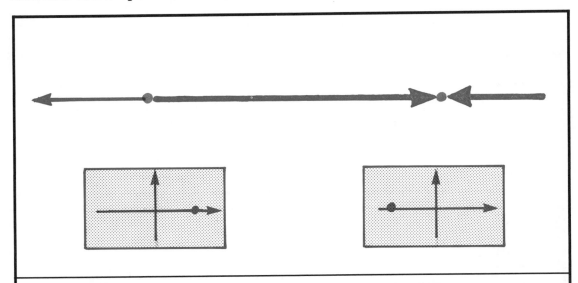

3.1.2. BEFORE: Here is a relatively simple phase portrait of a dynamical system in 1D. As closed orbits are impossible, the only limit sets are critical points. Here there are only two of them. Their CEs, shown in the windows, are hyperbolic. This system is structurally stable. There is only one attractor, and its basin is shaded green. The repellor is the separatrix, and the outset consists of a trajectory going to infinity to the left. We could regard infinity as an attractor in this case, and the blue segment as its basin.

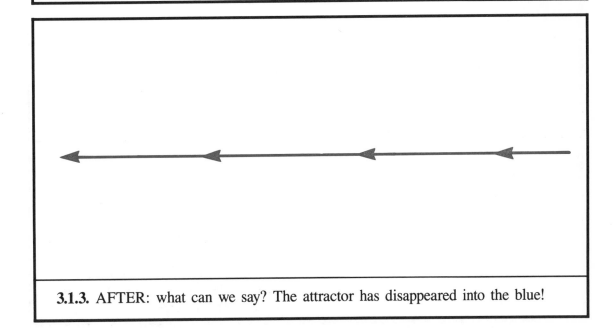

3.1.3. AFTER: what can we say? The attractor has disappeared into the blue!

How can we go smoothly from BEFORE to AFTER by simply turning a control knob? The clue, hinted in the first panel of this section, is in the CEs.

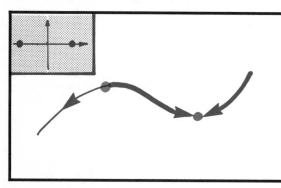

3.1.4. Here is BEFORE again, but we have bent the state space so that the flow of the dynamical system may be understood as raindrops trickling downhill. A puddle collects at the point attractor. The CEs are shown in the windows.

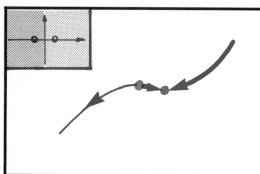

3.1.5. Pulling up the right hand end of the hill a bit brings the two critical points closer together: the red moth approaches the blue flame. The puddle decreases. Note that the CEs are getting intimate as well.

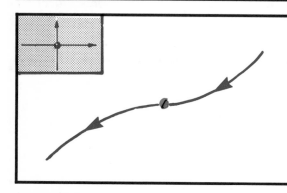

3.1.6. Pulling on the right end some more, the puddle and the two critical points are gone. The catastrophe has occurred!

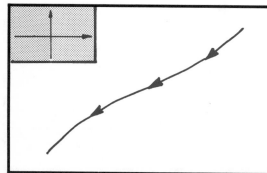

3.1.7. Pulling firmly up on the right end some more inreases the slope a bit, but makes little difference to the surface water. All rain goes downhill to the left forever.

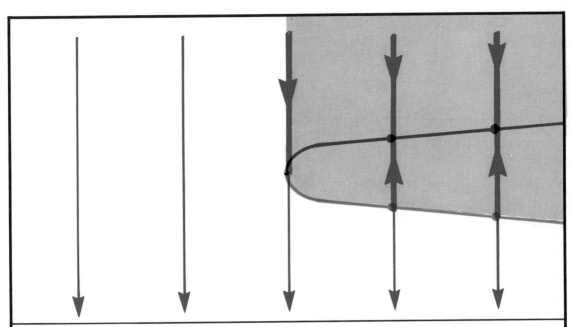

3.1.8. We now turn these phase portraits upright, place them side-by-side in their proper places in the response diagram of the dynamical scheme we have constructed, and interpolate a few more portraits. At the moment of bifurcation the red and green critical points meet at an inflection point of the curve (state space).

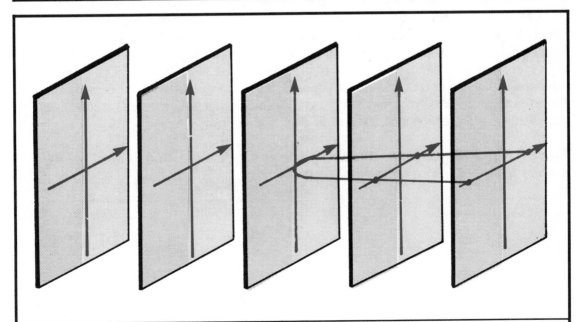

3.1.9. Plotting both of the blue CEs in the same red/green CE plane directly under the corresponding state space, we obtain this curve as a record of their dependence on the control parameter.

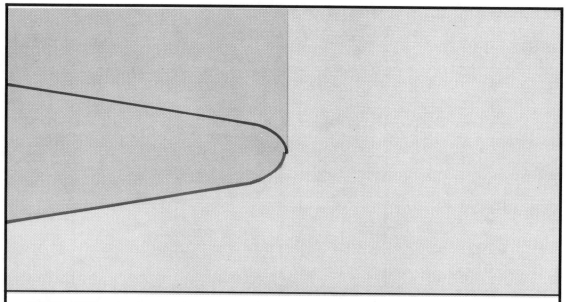

3.1.10. Filling in the continuous locus of each critical point as the control knob is smoothly changed provides this parabolic curve, the full response diagram of the static fold catastrophe in 1D.

Elementary catastrophe theory (ECT) is a beautiful subject, crucially important for the progress of many scientific subjects. Also, it boasts several superb expository texts, which are largely responsible for the development of the basic bifurcation concepts presented in this volume [2]. Study of the early chapters of these texts is strongly suggested for those who wish eventually to understand this atlas of bifurcations. BEWARE: Most of ECT deals with schemes having two or more control parameters, a context well beyond our present purview. But as our agreed context includes more complicated attractors than ECT allows, we will see challenging complications, even with only one control.

There is a growing literature of multiparameter bifurcations, and in due time we may present a pictorial atlas of some of them.

3.2. STATIC FOLD IN 2D

Here we present not a new bifurcation, but simply a review of the preceding event in a different context: a 2D state space. We will use the characterization of a critical point in 2D in terms of its CEs, as summarized in *Part Two,* Fig. 1.4.8. Again we are looking for the drift of a point attractor towards a fatal assignation with its separatrix. In 2D, recall that a separatrix must be either a periodic repeller or the inset of a saddle point. It is the latter case which occurs here.

In this event the point attractor drifts towards the saddle point of its separatrix.

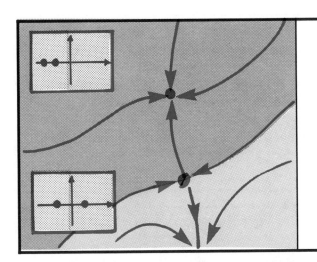

3.2.1. BEFORE: There are two critical points, a saddle (red/green) and an attractor (red). The inset of the saddle (green) is the separatrix of the basin of the attractor. The CEs are shown in the windows.

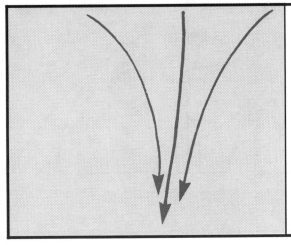

3.2.2. AFTER: There are no attractors, except for an infinite ocean in the South. All trajectories disappear into the blue. Note that a test droplet resting in equilibrium at the attractor before the event now finds itself in the blue basin of infinity, very far from equilibrium. It must now get underway and begin a major journey. This is the reason for the name, *catastrophe,* used in French to describe this behavior.

The mechanism of this event may be intuited from the fold in 1D. Just imagine the two critical points on a North/South train track, which is attractive to trajectories off the track to the East and West.

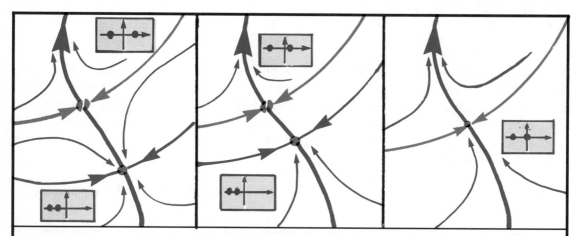

3.2.3. As the control knob is adjusted, let the two critical points fold together along the track, exactly as in the 1D event of the preceding section, culminating at the instant of bifurcation. But in this case there are *two* CEs for each of the two critical points. Only one of the CEs for each of the critical points is affected by the variation of the control. The affected CE corresponds to the strength of attraction or repulsion along the track. The other CE of each critical point indicates the attraction of the track for trajectories off the track, and is unaffected by the control. At the moment of catastrophe, there is only one critical point, and it is nonhyperbolic, as one of its CEs is zero.

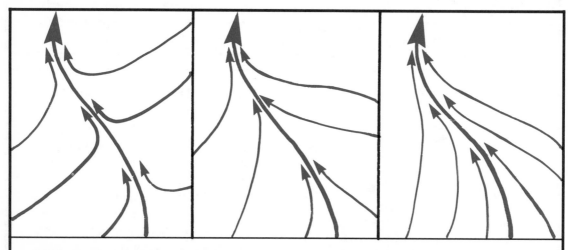

3.2.4. As the control knob continues to turn, the nonhyperbolic critical point vanishes into the blue, and the flow smooths over the shadow of the event.

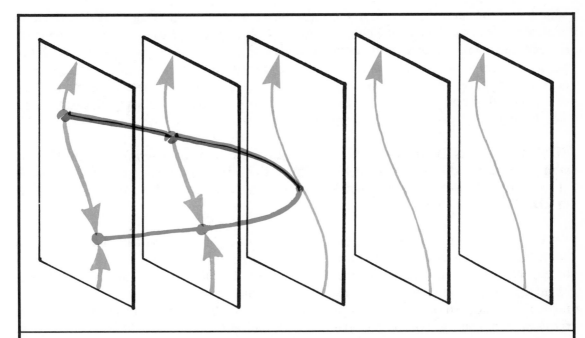

3.2.5. Erecting the six phase portraits side-by-side in their proper positions in the space of the response diagram, we obtain this skeleton of the full response of the scheme.

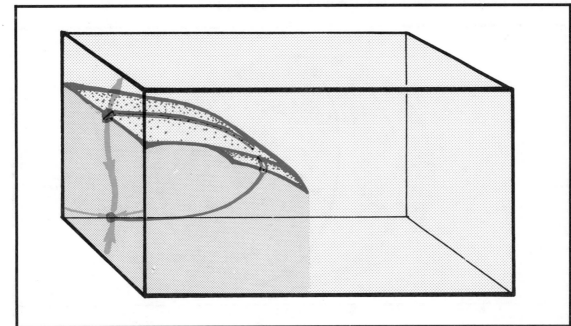

3.2.6. Interpolating the remaining details, we have this cut-away picture of the full response diagram.

Note that if the control is moved to the right, the catastrophe may be described as the drift of an attractor to a saddle point within its separatrix. At contact, there occurs the simultaneous disappearance into the blue of three things: the attractor, its entire separatrix, and its entire basin. But reading from right to left, the catastrophic event consists of an increasingly evident slowing down of the blue flow in a certain region, then the magical emergence (out of the blue slow region) of an attractor, with its full-blown basin and separatrix. Thus, the fold is sometimes called an *annihilation/creation event.*

SUMMARY: This 2D version of the fold is may be called the *extension* of the 1D version presented in the preceding section. This is the same relationship that we have seen at the end of the preceding chapter, in which the octave jump event was presented first in 2D, then again in 3D.

We want to point out, before going on to another event, that the bifurcation events we are describing one at a time in small boxes of euclidean space are *atomic events.* They are to be expected, in actual dynamical schemes encountered in applications, in molecular combinations comprising complex response diagrams, such as that of the stirring machine. A further complication encountered in practice is that the phase portrait of the system, for a fixed value of control, will be a global one with multiple attractors and basins. Generally, at a given bifurcation, only a small part of the global picture will affected. Our atomic response diagrams may thus be encountered in a small piece of the garden variety response diagram.

Here is a global version of the 2D fold catastrophe. As usual with catastrophic events, the total number of basins is altered by the bifurcation.

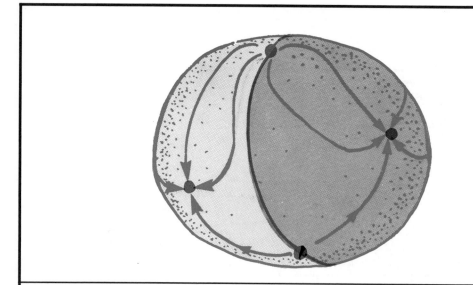

3.2.7. BEFORE: A flow on the two-sphere has two basins. Each attractor is static. The separatrix is the inset of a saddle point, completed by a repellor at the North Pole.

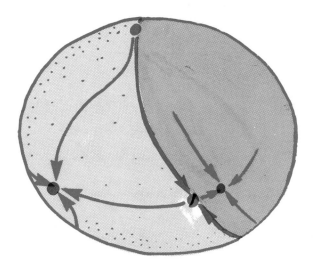

3.2.8 APPROACHING: One of the attractors has drifted close to the separatrix. Near the other attractor, nothing has changed.

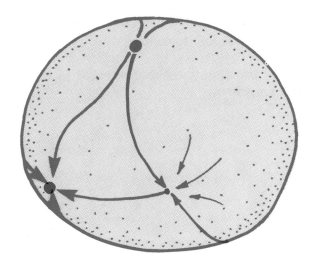

3.2.9. BIFURCATION INSTANT: Briefly, there is a degenerate (nonhyperbolic) critical point on the separatrix, which is now virtual, within the basin of the one-and-only attractor.

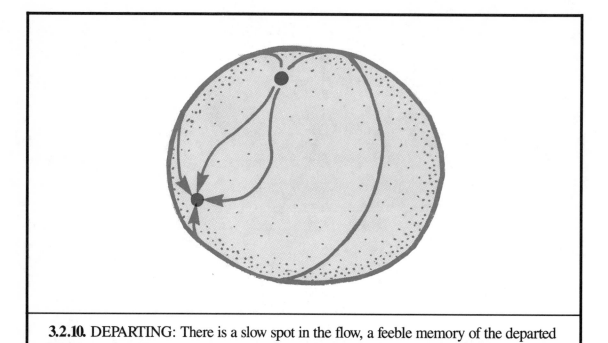

3.2.10. DEPARTING: There is a slow spot in the flow, a feeble memory of the departed basin.

A response diagram for this scheme is easy to imagine, but difficult to draw. Only the study of numerous examples of real systems, such as are found in the literature of experimental and applied dynamics, can give an idea of the enormous variety of response diagrams which may be constructed from the atomic bifurcations which we have presented so far.

But furthermore, some of the atomic events presented in the following drawings get pretty complicated by themselves.

3.3. PERIODIC FOLD IN 2D

The fold catastrophe we have seen in the two preceding sections for static attractors has an analogue for periodic attractors. One way to understand this periodic fold catastophe is by a rotation of the static fold in 1D around a circle.

We now depart the domain of elementary catastrophe theory forever.

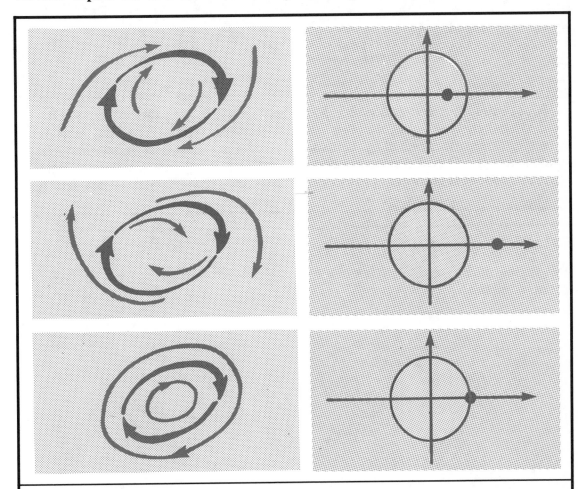

3.3.1. Recall the characterisation of a limit cycle in 2D by means of its CM. Here is a table of three cases from *Part Two,* Fig. 2.2.7: attractor, repellor, and a highly degenerate intermediate case. The CMs on the right correspond to the limit cycles on the left.

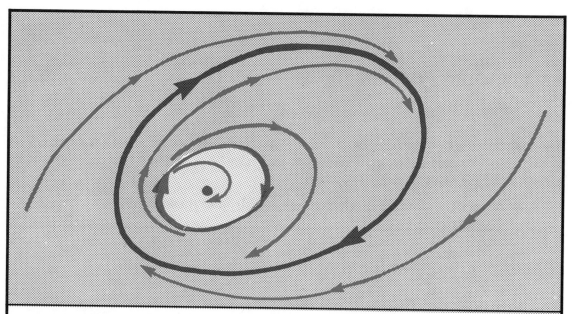

3.3.2. BEFORE: Here is a simple phase portrait in 2D, with two attractors. One is static (light blue basin), the other periodic (dark blue basin). A periodic repellor serves as separatrix, dividing the two basins. If a test droplet is thrown into this dynamic, it will evolve towards a rest state ('off') if it falls initially into the light blue, and toward oscillation ('on') if it falls to the dark blue. A toggle switch to turn on a motor might have a model of this *bistable* type.

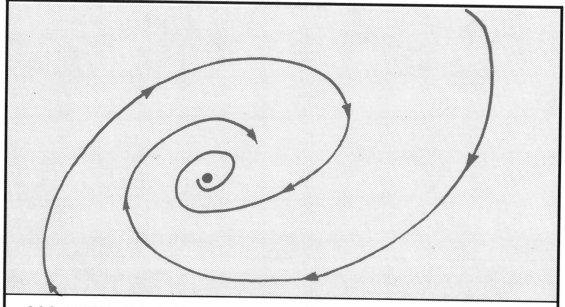

3.3.3. AFTER: This simpler phase portrait is *monostable*. Any initial state will settle to the 'off' attractor as its transient dies away.

The annihilation of the periodic attractor takes place in a periodic fold catastrophe.

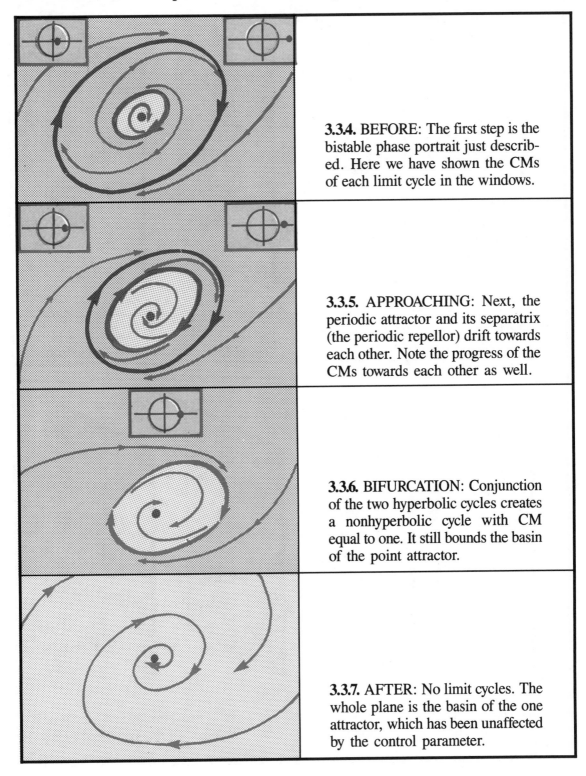

3.3.4. BEFORE: The first step is the bistable phase portrait just described. Here we have shown the CMs of each limit cycle in the windows.

3.3.5. APPROACHING: Next, the periodic attractor and its separatrix (the periodic repellor) drift towards each other. Note the progress of the CMs towards each other as well.

3.3.6. BIFURCATION: Conjunction of the two hyperbolic cycles creates a nonhyperbolic cycle with CM equal to one. It still bounds the basin of the point attractor.

3.3.7. AFTER: No limit cycles. The whole plane is the basin of the one attractor, which has been unaffected by the control parameter.

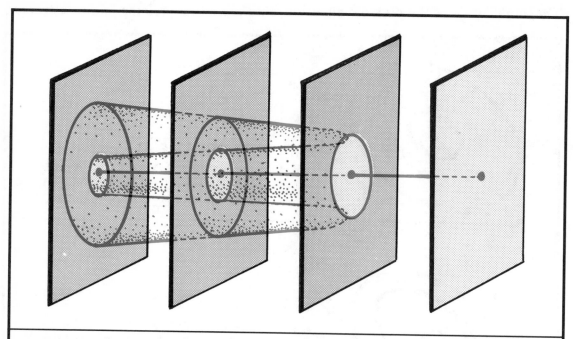

3.3.8. Here we stack the four phase portraits just described side-by-side in their proper positions in the response diagram of the hypothetical scheme under discussion.

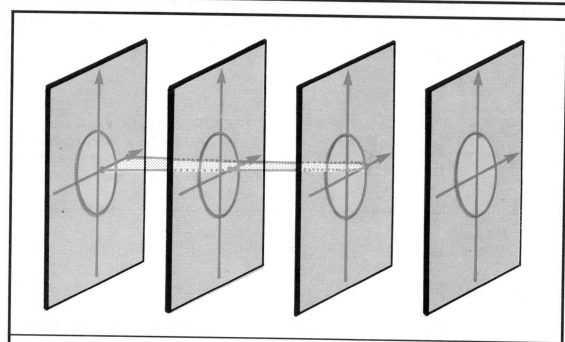

3.3.9. Here, suitably enlarged, we stack the CMs of the two limit cycles, this time in the same CM plane. Note the similarity to the CE movie of the static fold in 1D (Fig. 3.1.9).

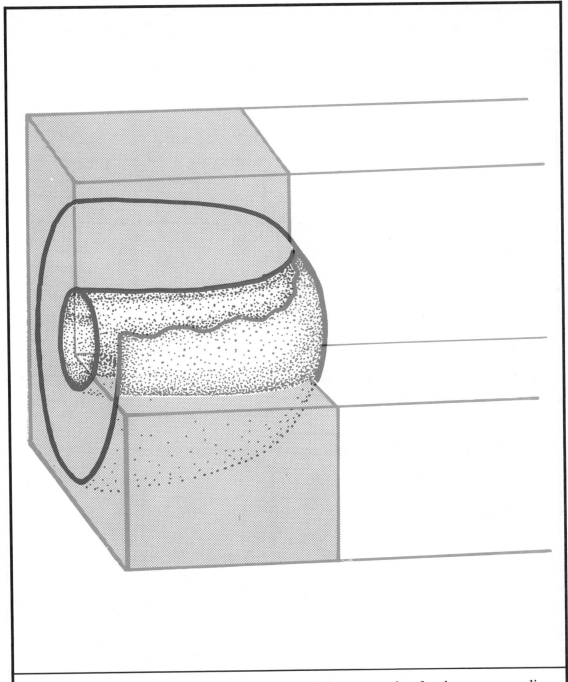

3.3.10. Finally, we interpolate a continuum of phase portraits, for the museum edition of the response diagram of this event. For easy viewing, we have omitted the blue filling denoting the locus of the blue basin. Also, we have omitted the static attractor in the center of the blue basin entirely, as it is not really part of this atomic bifurcation event.

For the response diagrams of bifurcations involving periodic attractors, it is is sometimes helpful (or even essential) to extract a strobe section movie of the entire event.

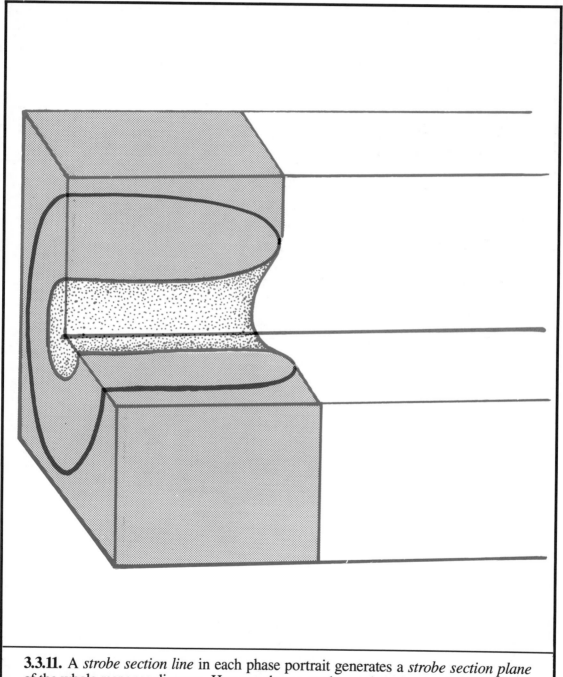

3.3.11. A *strobe section line* in each phase portrait generates a *strobe section plane* of the whole response diagram. Here we show a strobe section plane embedded within the whole response diagram as a vertical wall: the second riser of the figure's step shape.

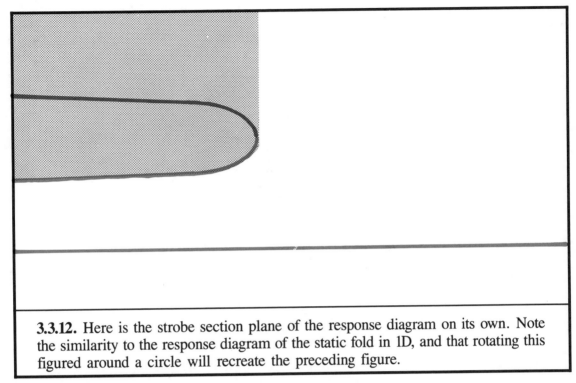

3.3.12. Here is the strobe section plane of the response diagram on its own. Note the similarity to the response diagram of the static fold in 1D, and that rotating this figured around a circle will recreate the preceding figure.

As in the fold catastrophe in 2D, we are going to illustrate this event in a more realistic global context.

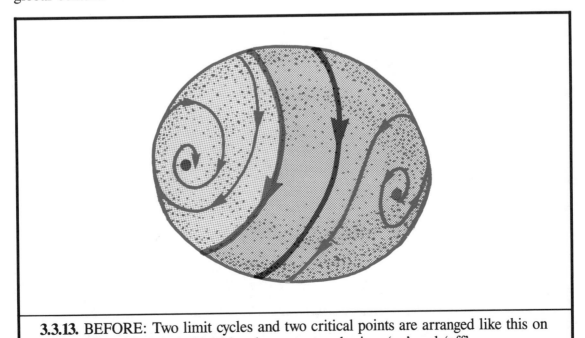

3.3.13. BEFORE: Two limit cycles and two critical points are arranged like this on the sphere. The flow is bistable: there are two basins, 'on' and 'off'.

3.3.14. APPROACHING: The 'on' attractor and its separatrix drift towards each other.

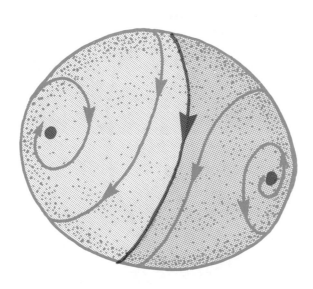

3.3.15. BIFURCATION: The conjunction of the two cycles creates a nonhyperbolic cycle, shown here as a thin red cycle.

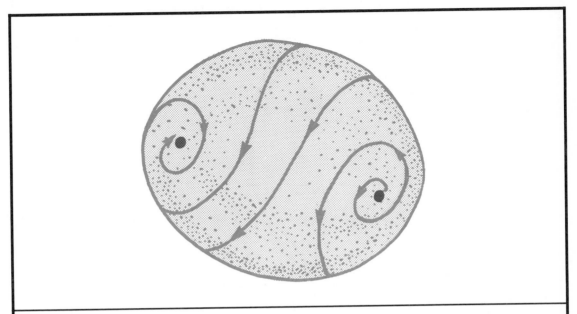

3.3.16. AFTER: The common monostable flow. The blue basin is greatly enlarged.

SUMMARY: This is a new entry for our encyclopedia, but it is very similar to the static fold. We now have five distinct atomic bifurcations on our list, in two categories:

Subtle — first excitation, second excitation, and octave jump.
Catastrophic — static fold, and periodic fold.

We continue now with another version of the periodic fold.

WARNING: A strobe section is not exactly revealed by a strobe light blinking periodically. By a strobe section, or Poincaré section, we mean simply a cross section of the flow.

3.4. PERIODIC FOLD IN 3D

This is not a new bifurcation for our list, but just another occurence of the periodic fold. This introduces not only a more general context for this bifurcation, but also some techniques of visual representation which we will find useful in the sequel.

We need to recall the basic concepts of limit cycles in 3D.

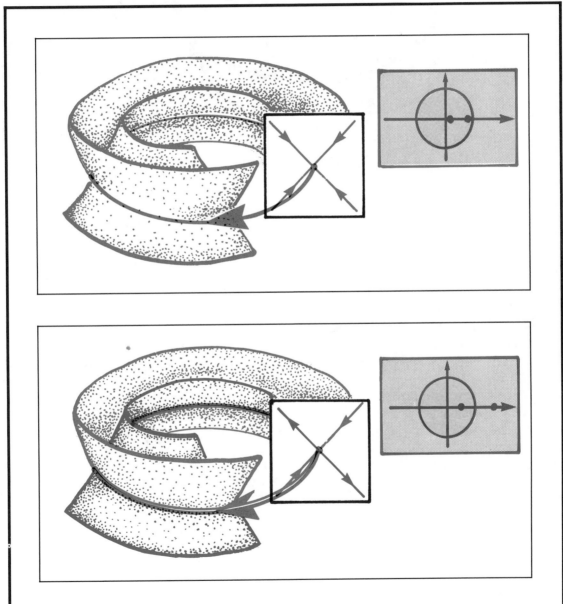

3.4.1. Here are two kinds of elementary limit cycles in 3D, along with their CMs, taken from *Part Two,* Fig. 2.5.7.

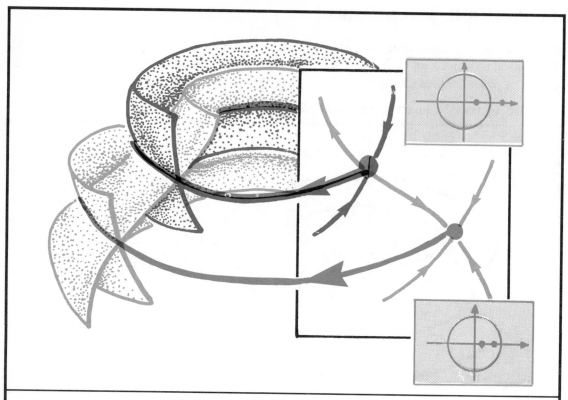

3.4.2. BEFORE: This is a portion of a flow in 3D, showing two elementary limit cycles—a saddle and an attractor—along with their CMs, and some discrete trajectories (the blue points, which belong to a continuously spiralling trajectory, are revealed by the strobe light) in the strobe section.

It will be easier to visualize this event by restricting attention to the strobe planes. But you must keep in mind that the dynamics within the strobe plane is *discrete*. That is, continuous trajectories of the 3D flow appear as a discrete sequence of points in the 2D strobe plane.

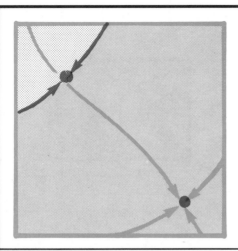
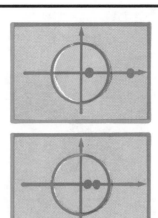

3.4.3. BEFORE, STROBED: Here is the initial configuration in the strobe plane. The green curve, the strobed inset of the saddle, is the boundary (within the strobe plane) of the strobed dark blue basin of the strobed periodic attractor (red point). The light blue region is the strobe view of the basin of some other attractor, which is out of sight.

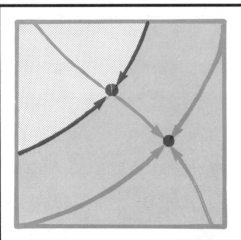
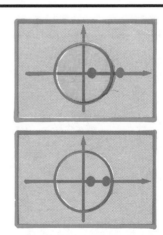

3.4.4. APPROACHING: The attractor and the saddle belonging to its separatrix move towards each other, as the control of the scheme is increased. At the same time, one of the CMs of the attractor (controlling the attraction in the North/South direction) moves outward toward the real number one on the unit circle in the CM plane. This indicates a *weakening* of the strength of attraction in this direction. The other CM of the attractor (controlling East/West attraction) is unaffected. Meanwhile the outer CM of the saddle (controlling North/South repulsion) moves inward toward the unit circle. The other CM of the saddle is unaffected.

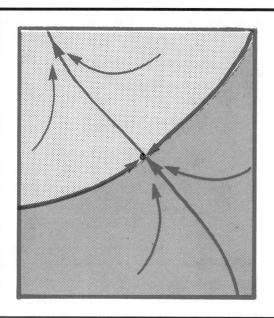

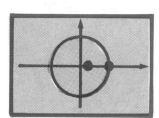

3.4.5. BIFURCATION: At the moment of conjunction, the two points (and the entire limit cycles they represent) coincide. This single limit cycle is nonhyperbolic, as one of its CMs is *one,* on the unit circle.

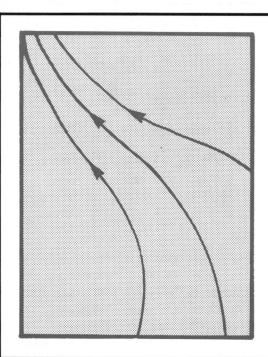

3.4.6. AFTER: No limit cycles. All points in the strobe plane belong to the blue basin.

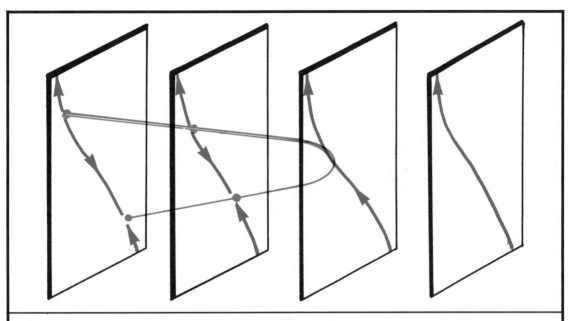

3.4.7. Here are the strobed portraits, erected side-by-side in their proper places within the (strobed) response diagram (recall Fig. 3.3.12). Note the parabolic meeting common to all of the fold catastrophes.

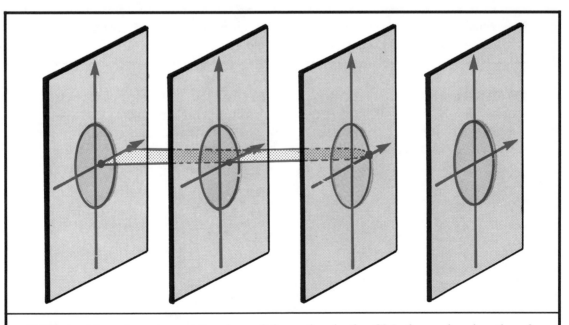

3.4.8. And here is a composite view of the action in the CM plane, showing the affected CMs of each limit cycle only. As the control moves to the right and the two limit cycles move towards each other, the two CMs approach *plus one* on the real axis. (Compare with 3.3.9.)

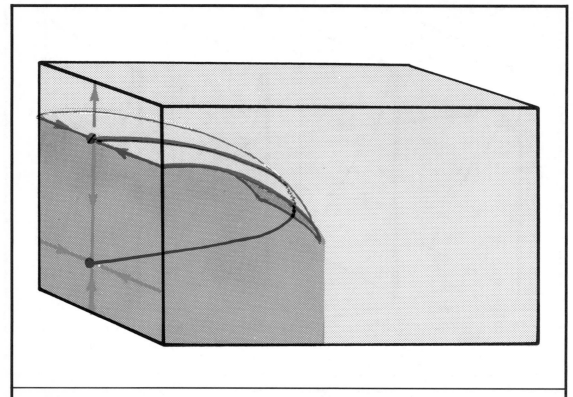

3.4.9. Finally, interpolation of a continuum of strobe planes in the strobed response diagram yields this memorable version (compare 3.2.6).

SUMMARY: This 3D version is harder to visualize than the 2D version of the periodic fold catastrophe. This atomic bifurcation may occur in 4D, and higher dimensions as well. Also, it may occur in much more complicated global phase portraits. It is particularly common in the dynamics of forced oscillators, as we have explained in *Part One*, Section 5.5.

4. PINCH CATASTROPHES

We now discover some new events for our atlas by reversing the direction of time. Thus, insets become outsets, attractors become repellors, and so on. In this chapter we systematically reverse the four subtle bifurcations of Chapter 2, obtaining a new catastrophe in each case.

4.1. SPIRAL PINCH IN 2D

We begin with the first excitation in 2D, otherwise known as the Hopf bifurcation. What happens when we reverse the direction of time?

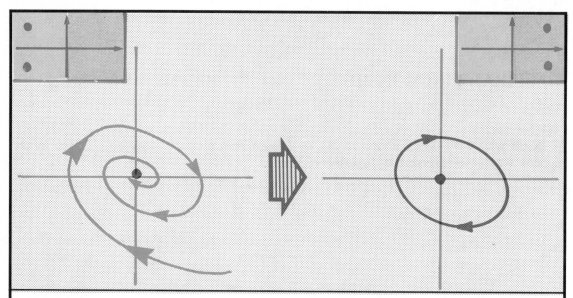

4.1.1. Recall, from Section 2.1, that in this event a point attractor of spiral type expands parabolically into a periodic attractor. The critical point turns into a point repellor of spiral type (a virtual separatrix) as its CEs transit the imaginary axis of the CE plane, from the red to the green region.

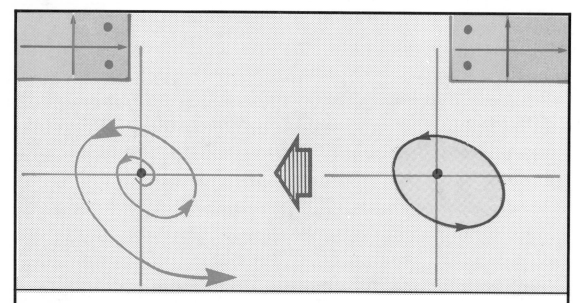

4.1.2. Reversing the direction of flow of all trajectories, we obtain a point repellor of spiral type on the left. We will take this portrait as the final one of the new event. On the right, a point attractor of spiral type is surrounded by a periodic repellor, the actual separatrix of its basin (blue). We will consider this one the initial portrait of this event.

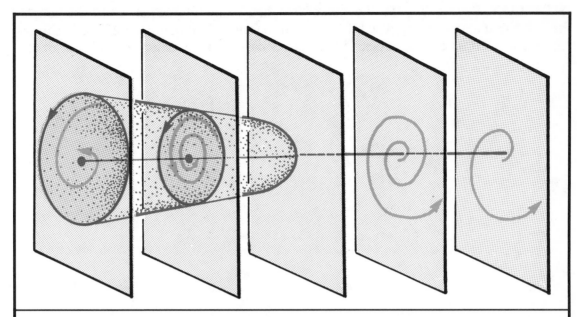

4.1.3. Erecting these portraits in their proper positions in the response diagram and interpolating a few others, we obtain this side-by-side skeleton.

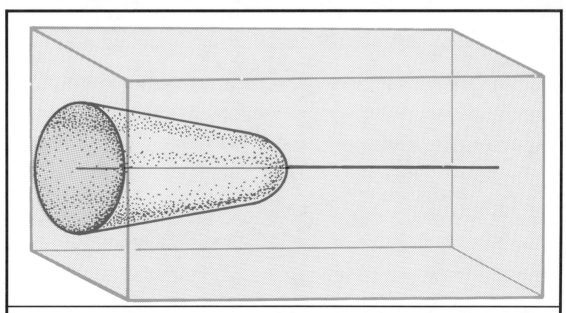

4.1.4. Stripping off the CE details and shading in the continuous locus of attraction, we obtain this image of the spiral pinch event in 2D. Note that as the control is increased to the right, the separatrix (and basin) shrinks down to the point attractor, the strength of which is dwindling as well. At the moment of bifurcation, the actual separatrix becomes a virtual separatrix, replacing the point attractor, which has catastrophically vanished.

SUMMARY: By reversing the direction of flow in a subtle bifurcation, first excitation, we have obtained a new catastrophic bifurcation for our atlas. The spiralling 2D basin shrinks, and pinches off its central attractor. Separatrix, basin, and attractor all vanish at once.

4.2. VORTICAL PINCH IN 3D

Reversing direction in first excitation was easy, so we will repeat the operation for the second excitation. Once again, time reversal will create a catastrophe from a subtle bifurcation.

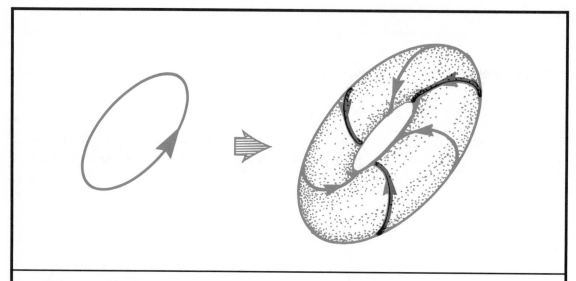

4.2.1. Recall this event in 3D from Section 2.2, in which a periodic attractor is transformed into a periodic repellor within a braided AIT.

Technically, this event is not a single bifurcation. Instead, it consists of a fractal family of bifurcations. As in Section 2.2, we will not dwell on this complication, which concerns the braid dynamics on the AIT, but just concentrate on the central cycle and the AIT.

And now, about face! Attractors become repellors, and so on.

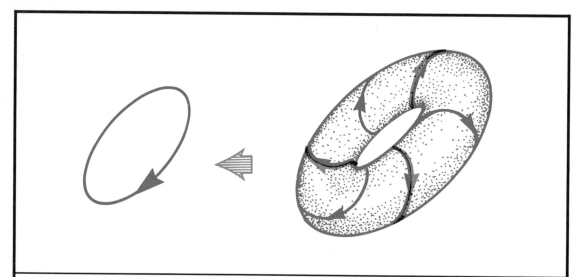

4.2.2. On the left, the periodic attractor of spiral type has become a repellor. And on the right, the attractive invariant torus (AIT) has become a repulsive invariant torus (RIT). As in the preceding section, we will regard the portrait on the right as the initial configuration.

Now let's strobe these portraits, to cut things down to 2D.

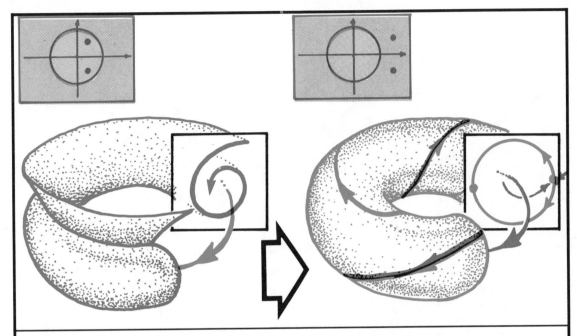

4.2.3. Here again is second excitation, showing the strobe plane, along with the CMs of the central cycle.

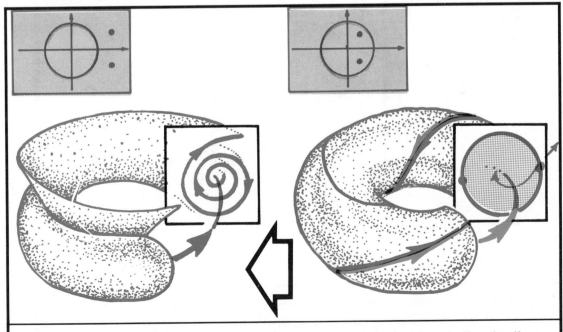

4.2.4. And here is the same portrait, with time reversed, showing similar details.

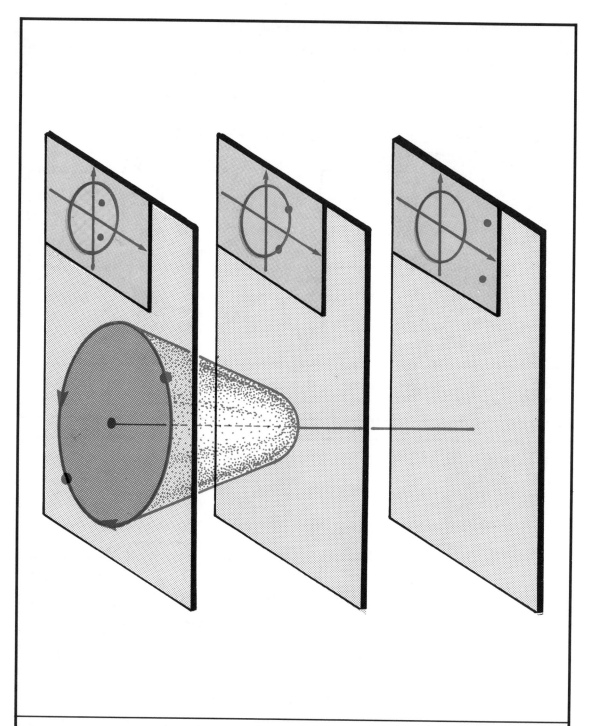

4.2.5. Erecting the two strobe plane portraits in their proper positions in the space of the strobed response diagram, and interpolating a few in-betweens, we have the skeleton of the strobed response diagram.

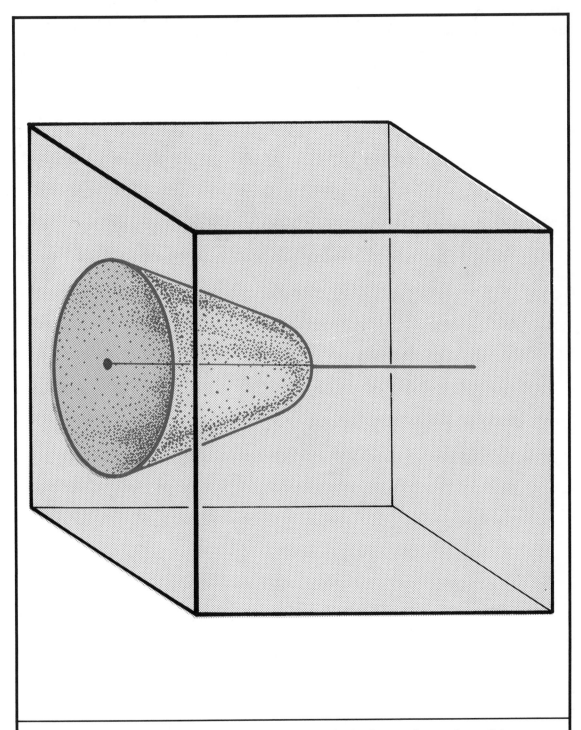

4.2.6. Stripping off the details and filling in the loci of attraction and repulsion, we have this framable image of the vortical basin pinching down to destroy its central attractor.

SUMMARY: Reversal of a subtle bifurcation has again given us a new catastrophe for our atlas of response diagrams of atomic bifurcation events. As long as there is an invariant torus in the portrait, we must expect a fractal set of braid bifurcations on it. But in this case, they do not affect the locus of attraction. The green RIT shrinks, and catastrophically pinches off the central periodic attractor, as the control is moved to the right.

4.3. OCTAVE PINCH IN 2D

Recall that the octave jump phenomenon involved a periodic attractor, as one of its CMs transits the unit circle at *minus one*. In the 2D version presented in Section 2.3, the affected limit cycle turns into a periodic repellor, and a period-doubled attractor is emitted. The state space is necessarily a Möbius band.

What happens to the octave jump if the direction of time is reversed?

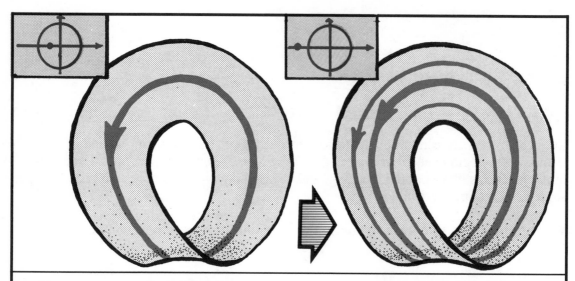

4.3.1. Here are the BEFORE and AFTER portraits, recalled from Section 2.3. Note that the basin is not substantially changed by the bifurcation, it is almost the entire band. After the event, the single-period repellor (green) is a *virtual separatrix*. This means that while technically it is a separatrix (that is, it does not belong to any basin), it does not actually separate two distinct basins. (See *Part One,* Section 1.5. and *Part Three,* Section 1.2.)

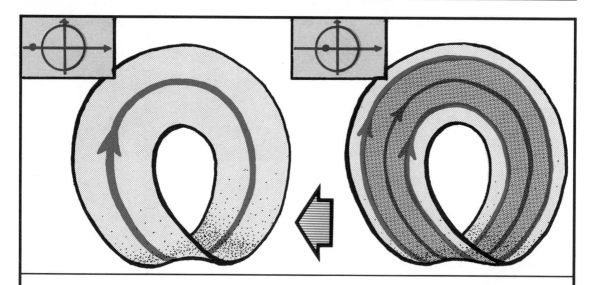

4.3.2. Reversing time, the flow goes backwards, and attraction is replaced by repulsion. On the left, we have a periodic repellor, as a virtual separatrix in the basin of an attractor out of view. On the right, we have a single-period attractor in the dark blue basin bounded by the double-period repellor, an actual separatrix. We will now regard the portrait on the right as the initial configuration.

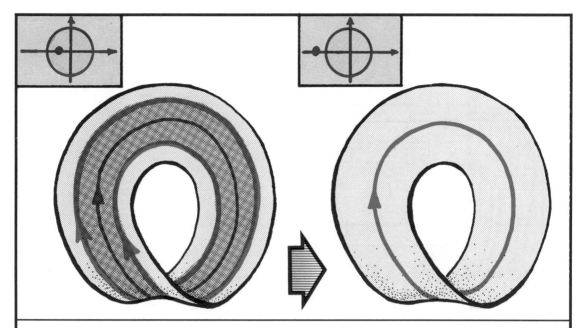

4.3.3. From this perspective, we see a periodic attractor disappear as the control parameter increases. The actual separatrix of the dark blue basin contracts towards its weakening attractor, and pinches the entire basin down to a meager repellor, and virtual separatrix. The CMs shown are for the central cycle only.

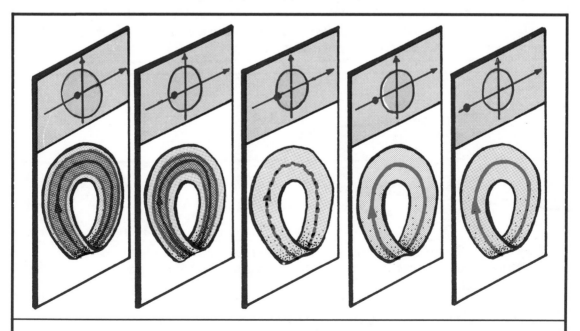

4.3.4. Erecting these two portraits into a side-by- side representation and interpolating three more, we obtain this skeleton of the octave pinch event.

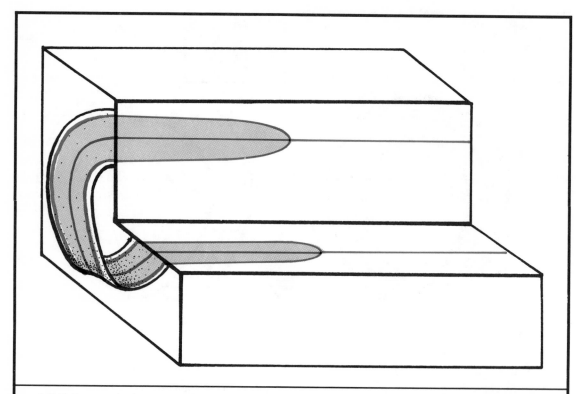

4.3.5. Interpolating a continuum, we fill out the skeleton to create this smoothed and cut-away response diagram. Here we have cut away a segment of the diagram for better viewing, and also to suggest the strobed response diagram, in which each full phase portrait is replaced by a strobe section line.

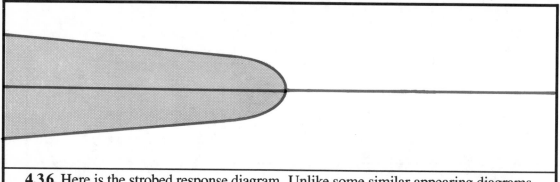

4.3.6. Here is the strobed response diagram. Unlike some similar appearing diagrams appearing earlier, the two branches of the green curve both correspond to the same periodic repellor.

SUMMARY: Running the 2D octave jump backwards yields a new entry for our atlas of generic bifurcations with one control. This is our third example of a pinching catastrophe. The basin and separatrix of a periodic attractor shrink, and eventually pinch off the attractor, leaving a green shadow (periodic repellor) in its place.

4.4. OCTAVE PINCH IN 3D

As we have seen earlier, an atomic bifurcation event may present itself in contexts of different dimension. Nevertheless, we may regard these presentations as essentially the same event. One way to increase the dimension of a presentation is to embed the phase portraits in a larger state space as an attractive, invariant subspace. We have referred to this previously as the *extension* construction. For example, the octave jump in 3D is the extension of the octave jump in 2D.

Similarly, the octave pinch in 2D may be extended to obtain the octave pinch in 3D.

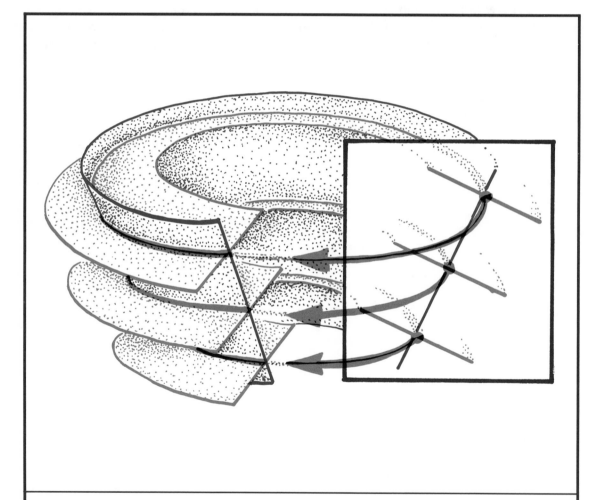

4.4.1. BEFORE: Here is the initial portrait of the 2D octave pinch, from 4.1.3 , embedded as an attractive blue band in a 3D flow. The single-periodic attractor within the 2D context becomes a single-periodic 3D attractor after the embedding. But the double-periodic repellor of the 2D band becomes a double-periodic saddle after the embedding, as it is attractive in the North/South direction, but repelling in the East/West direction.

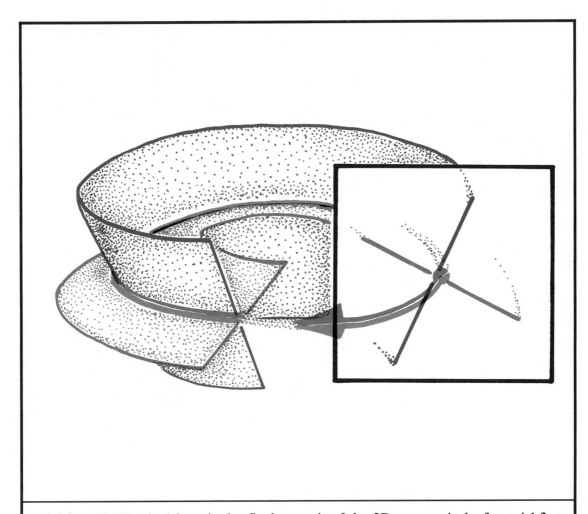

4.4.2. AFTER: And here is the final portrait of the 2D octave pinch, from 4.1.3, as the same blue band. The attraction of the 3D flow to the blue band is unaffected by the control parameter. The single-periodic repellor of the 2D band becomes, after embedding, a single-periodic saddle.

We may create space for the indication of additional detail by extracting the strobe sections.

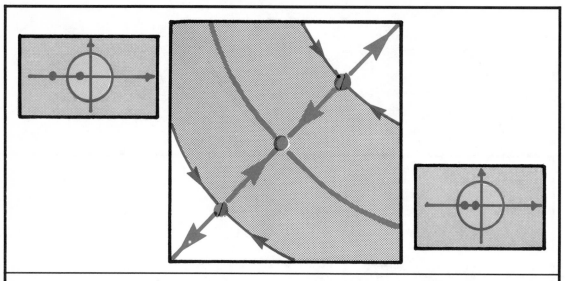

4.4.3. BEFORE: Here is the strobe section plane of the initial 3D flow. The inset band of the saddle (green) cuts the section in two disjoint line segments. These comprise the actual separatrix of the blue basin of the central attractor. The CMs of each limit cycle are shown in their own windows.

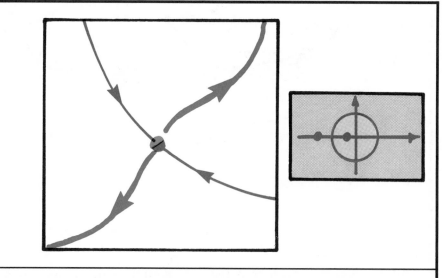

4.4.4. AFTER: Here is the strobe plane of the final portrait, showing the CMs of the solitary limit cycle. The inset is a virtual separatrix, all that remains of the former attractor, basin, and actual separatrix, after the pinch.

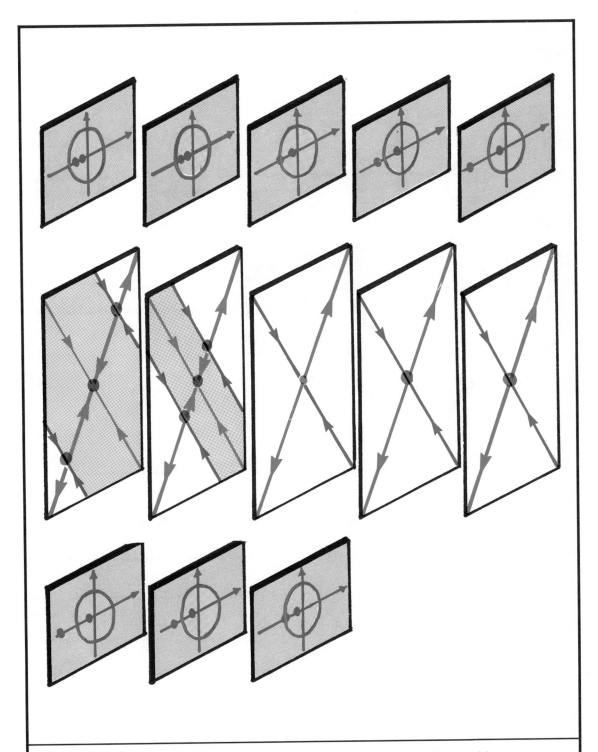

4.4.5. Erecting these portraits with interpolations, we have the side-by-side representation of the response diagram of the 3D octave pinch.

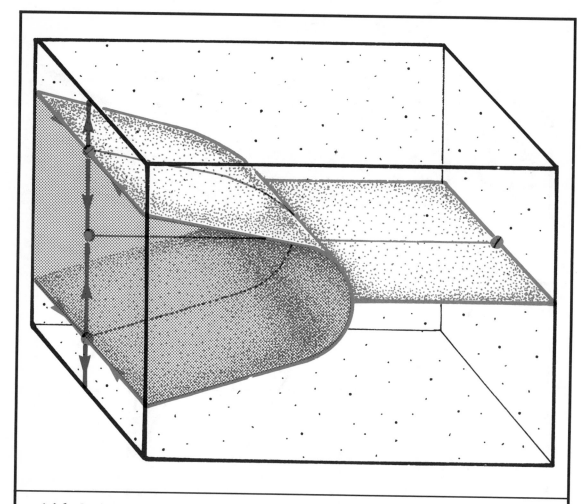

4.4.6. Omitting details and smoothing in the interpolations gives us this cut-away representation for the gallery.

SUMMARY: The 3D octave pinch is not a new entry for the encyclopedia of bifurcations, but simply another presentation of the 2D pinch. Again, a basin pinches down to a virtual separatrix, and its attractor is catastrophically lost.

5. SADDLE CONNECTION BIFURCATIONS

This is the third and final chapter on catastrophic bifucations. The fold and pinching bifurcations are rather similar types. In a *fold,* an attractor drifts toward its separatrix, where it collides with a peer, a similar actor. In a *pinch,* a separatrix squeezes down on an attractor, and the collision involves dissimilar actors. But both types are *local* events: the action takes place in the immediate neighborhood of the affected attractor. We are now going to consider some *global* bifurcations, in which the tangling of insets and outsets create large-scale consequences. The concepts of global behavior from *Part Three* will be indispensable.

5.1. BASIN BIFURCATION IN 2D

We have encountered this phenomenon previously, under the name *saddle switching,* in *Part Three,* Fig. 4.1.1. The structural instability, at the moment of bifurcation, is caused by the violation of *generic condition G3* by a *saddle connection* in 2D (see *Part Three,* Section 2.1.).

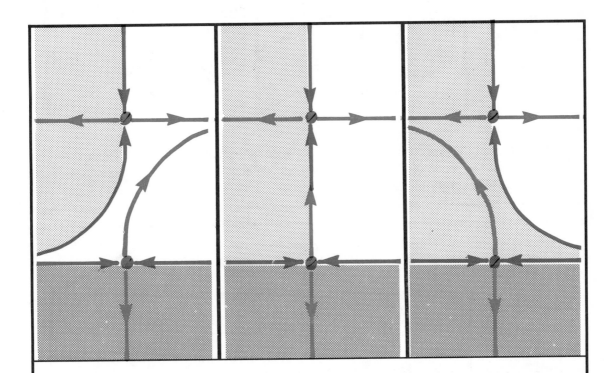

5.1.1. Here are the BEFORE, DURING, and AFTER shots of the event. There is not a single attractor in sight, although three are implied out-of-view. Portions of the three basins of attraction are shown (dark blue, light blue, and white regions). The insets of the saddles (green curves) comprise the separatrices. In this scheme, only one side of one inset and one side of one outset are affected by the conrol knob.

The effect of the bifurcation (passing through a saddle connection of *heteroclinic* type, that is, connecting two different saddle points) is to radically change the territory claimed by the two competing attractors. As only the basins are affected, and not the attractors, we call this a *basin bifurcation.*

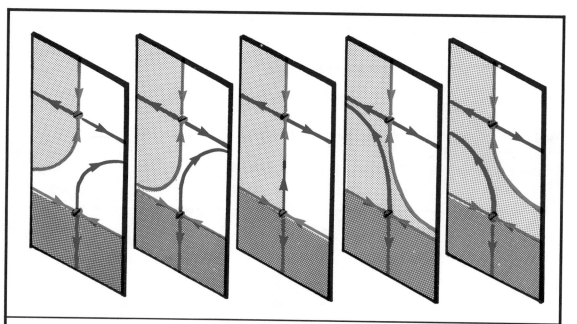

5.1.2. Erecting these portraits, and two in-between interpolations, in their proper positions within the space of the response diagram creates this side-by-side skeleton of the response diagram of this event.

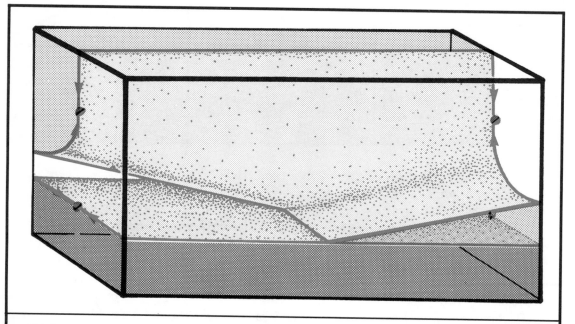

5.1.3. And shading in a continuum of other portraits, we have this cut-away version of the response diagram.

We may understand the effect of this event better in the context of an example. Recall the magnetic pendulum from *Part One,* Figs. 2.1.20 and 2.1.22, remembering that position in the figure indicates position *and speed* of the pendulum.

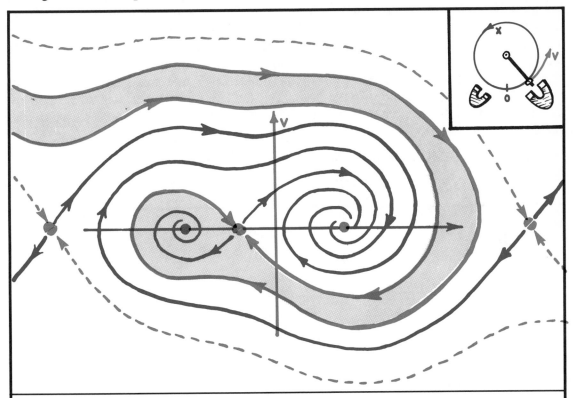

5.1.4. BEFORE: Here is the unrolled phase portrait of the machine in the window. The saddle points indicated on the extreme right and left both represent the same state, with the pendulum near the top of its swing. We will call this the *top saddle.* The insets, the solid green curves, are actual separatrices, while the dashed green curves represent virtual separatrices. The blue curves are outsets.

Note that the shaded basin winds around the cylinder indefinitely towards the North (upper half-plane).

In this phase portrait, the upper half cylinder (here shown unrolled, hence, the upper half plane) corresponds to counter-clockwise (CCW) rotation of the bob. If you want to spin the bob rapidly CCW and to have it fall eventually into the attractor of the smaller magnet on the left, you must start with an initial CCW spin and angle within the shaded basin. As this basin winds around the cylindrical state space (here shown unrolled) indefinitely while tending toward larger and larger CCW rotation rates, there are many good choices (for a given initial position, such as the top) for the initial CCW rate and for any initial CCW rate, there are starting positions in the basin. But for CW rates (lower half cylinder) there is only one small portion of the basin, and you must start within this small region to end up at the left equilibrium.

Thus, the probability of throwing the bob CW at random and having it end up at the left equilibrium is much smaller than it is in the CCW case.

5.1.5. Recall from *Part One,* Figs. 2.1.19, 2.3.18, 2.3.19 that friction determines the CEs, and thus the rate of decay of each spiralling trajectory, on the way to its attractor. On the left, here, is a closeup of one of the attractors in the case of strong friction. And on the right, the same attractor with weak friction.

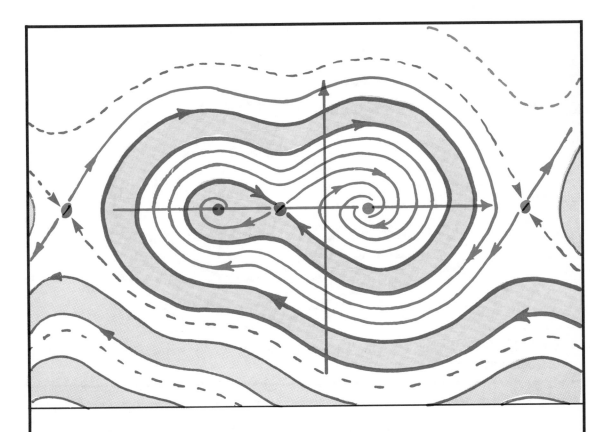

5.1.6. AFTER: Here is the phase portrait of the same pendulum system, with the friction in the hinge substantially reduced by a good lubrication. The key to the difference is the overall rate of spiralling toward the *bottom complex,* the configuration at the bottom of the swing (two point attractors and one saddle point). In fact, we might just pretend for a moment that the entire shaded basin is a single blue trajectory, attracted to this bottom complex. With less friction, more spirals are necessary to make a given amount of progress toward the bottom.

Note that the shaded basin of the equilibrium of the smaller magnet on the left now winds around the cylinder indefinitely toward the South. Surely this makes a difference, especially if you are left-handed. The probability of throwing the bob CW at random and having it end up at the left equilibrium is *much larger* than it is in the CCW case. We will now interpolate from BEFORE to AFTER through four in-betweens. The control parameter in this scheme will be the friction within the support axle of the pendulum, which will *decrease* during the sequence. Two occurrences of the saddle connection bifurcation will be discovered in the process.

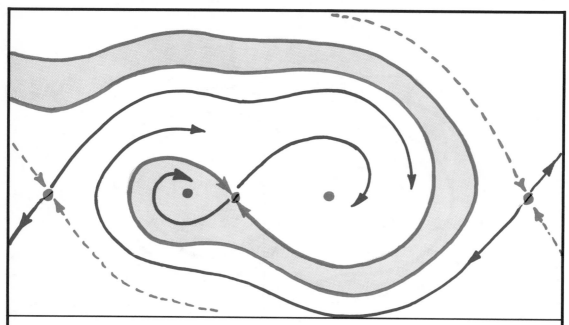

5.1.7. BEFORE: Strong friction. The system is structurally stable, and the tail of the blue snake winds to the North.

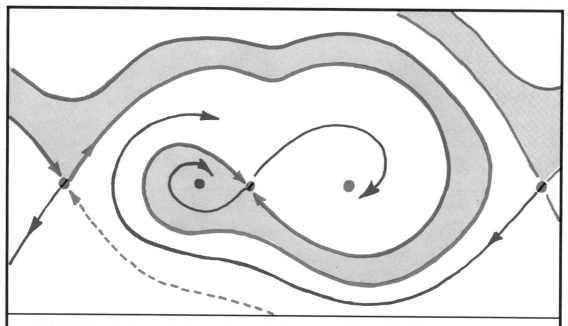

5.1.8. FIRST CONNECTION: After the first lubrication, the lower green boundary of the blue tail (half of the inset of the bottom saddle) makes contact with the blue outset of the top saddle (shown on the left) in a heteroclinic saddle connection. This is the first occurrence of basin bifurcation in this sequence of experiments.

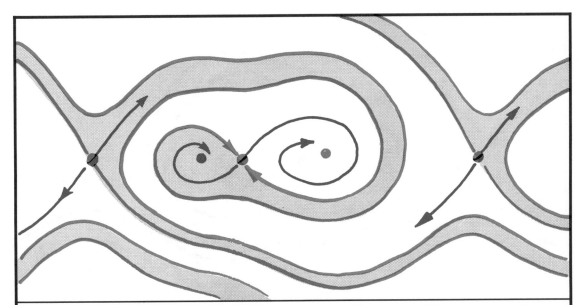

5.1.9. MIDDLE: After the second lubrication, the first basin bifurcation is behind us, the system is again structurally stable, and the blue tail is split into two streamers. There are good chances of hitting the blue basin with either CW or CCW spins. The lower half of the inset of the top saddle (shown on the left) has changed from a virtual to an actual separatrix.

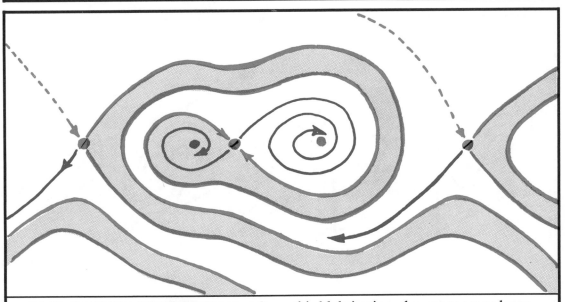

5.1.10. SECOND CONNECTION: After a third lubrication, the upper green boundary ot the blue tail conjoins the outset of the top saddle, the upper streamer of the blue basin has been pinched off, and the upper inset of the top saddle has switched from an actual to a virtual separatrix. This is the second occurrence of basin bifurcation in this sequence of experiments.

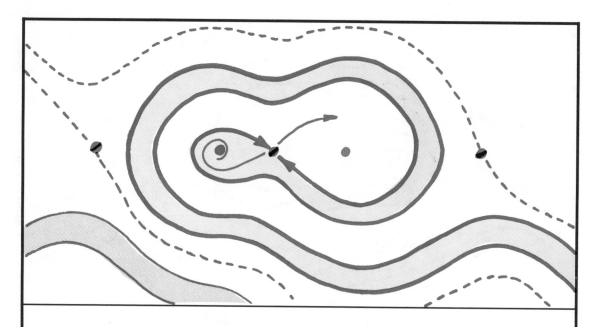

5.1.11. AFTER: After a final lubrication, the friction is reduced, the system is again structurally stable, and the blue tail winds only to the South.

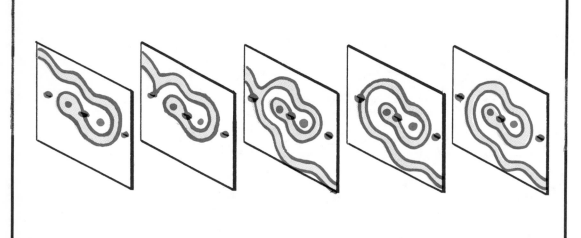

5.1.12. Erecting the five phase portraits in the space of the response diagram of this scheme, we have this side-by-side skeleton sketch.

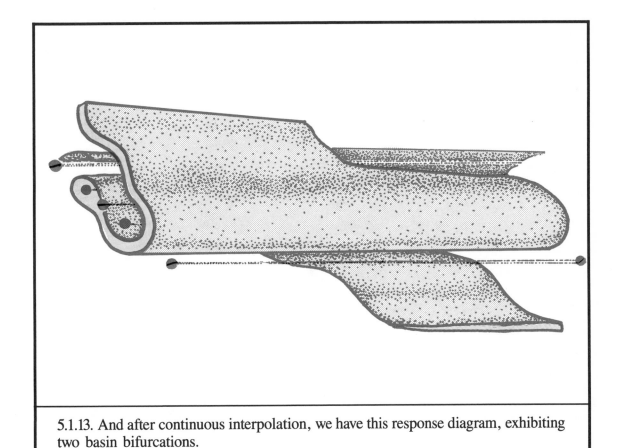

5.1.13. And after continuous interpolation, we have this response diagram, exhibiting two basin bifurcations.

SUMMARY: The saddle connection in 2D is the simplest basin bifurcation. There are numerous other simple examples, in all dimensions. But most saddle connection events in 3D or more entail further complications involving tangles, as we shall see later in this chapter.

5.2. PERIODIC BLUE SKY IN 2D

Saddle connections come in two sorts: heteroclinic and homoclinic. The latter are a much richer source of bifurcation behavior, as we shall now see.

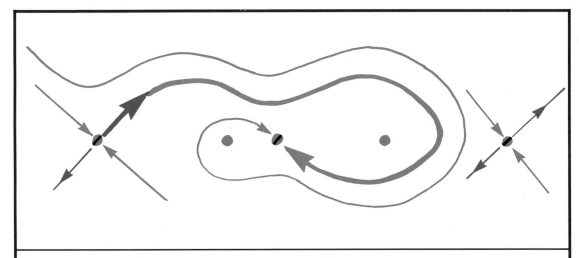

5.2.1. Recall this heteroclinic saddle connection from Fig. 5.1.8. What if this connection went from a saddle point to itself?

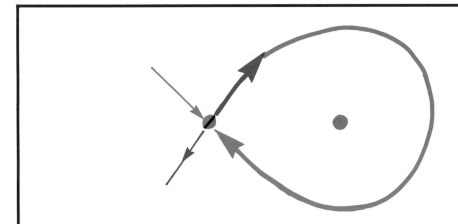

5.2.2. DURING: Here is a homoclinic saddle point in 2D. The outset to the North is conjunct with the inset from the East. This loop is a single trajectory of the flow. It is coming asymptotically from, and going asymptotically to, one and the same critical point. This portrait is not structurally stable. Enclosed within the loop must be, for topological reasons, at least one critical point.

Now let us try to embed this portrait in a bifurcation sequence.

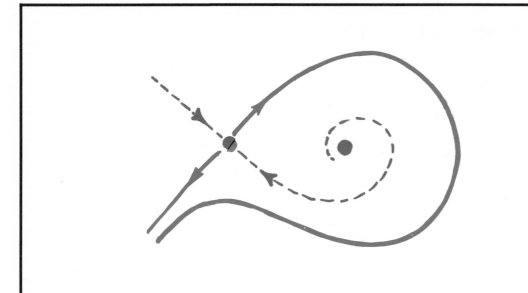

5.2.3. BEFORE: Here is a similar portrait, which is structurally stable. There are two critical points in view, a saddle and a repellor. The inset of the saddle is a virtual separatrix, in the basin of an out-of-sight attractor.

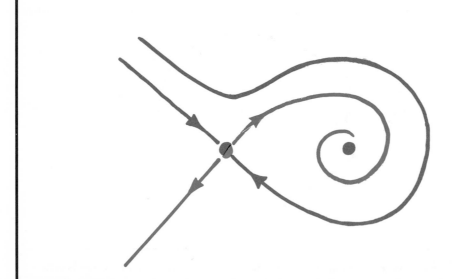

5.2.4. AFTER? If the control parameter steers the outset and inset curves which surround the repellor until they cross, as in Fig. 5.2.2, we might expect to end up with this portrait. But something is wrong here. The North-Eastern outset goes to a repellor!

Unless the repellor cleverly changed itself into an attractor at the very moment of the homoclinic conjunction, which is not allowed in the one-at-a-time style of a generic bifurcation, this portrait is impossible.

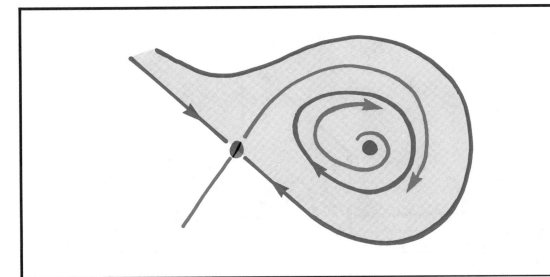

5.2.5. AFTER! Instead, what we find in the generic occurrence of this global bifurcation is the emission of a periodic attractor (of very long period) by the homoclinic conjunction. It simply appears *out of the blue*. The inset of the saddle changes from a virtual to an actual separatrix, and bounds the basin of the new attractor. The repellor is unaffected by the event.

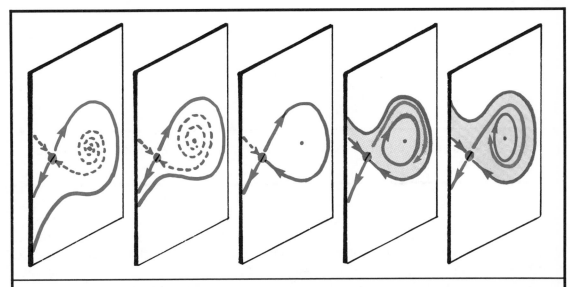

5.2.6. Putting the correct three portraits together with two in-betweens, we obtain this side-by-side skeleton of the response diagram.

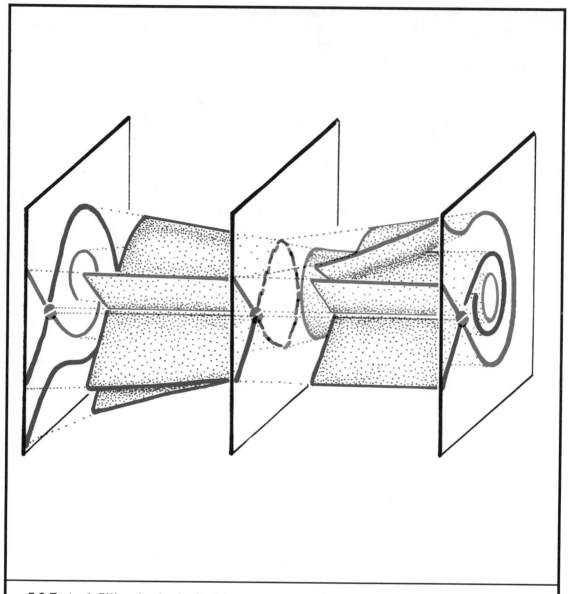

5.2.7. And filling in the loci of insets and outsets smoothly, we obtain this picture of the blue sky catastrophe.

SUMMARY: In this event, the momentary saddle connection is responsible for the appearance out of the blue of a slow, long-periodic attractor, and its large basin. This is a basin catastrophe, in that the basin jumps out fully formed, as well as the attractor. As the event is observed in reverse, the periodic attractor moves toward a certain segment of its separatrix, and they vanish into the blue together. As in a fold catastrophe, there is no pinching of the basin.

5.3. CHAOTIC BLUE SKY IN 3D

The suspension of the periodic blue sky event is not a straightforward construction, because a homoclinic saddle cycle in 3D involves a tangle of inset and outset surfaces *(Part Three,* Section 5.1), rather than the simple coincidence of inset and outset curves in 2D which we have seen in the preceding section. A fuller description of this event will be attempted in a later chapter, but here we introduce the basic event: a chaotic attractor (the Birkhoff bagel, see *Part Two,* Section 3.2) appears out of the blue.

The initial and final portraits of this event are obtained from those of the 2D periodic blue sky event by simply swinging them around a cycle.

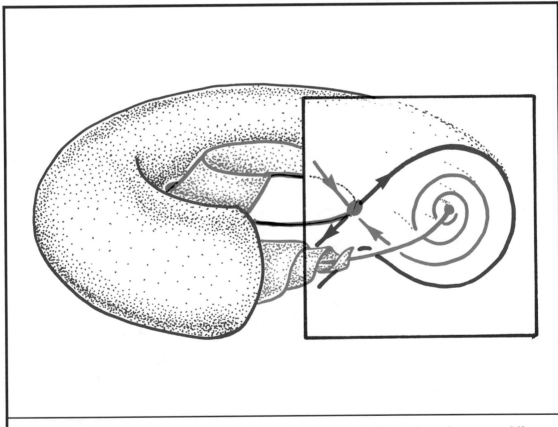

5.3.1. BEFORE: This phase portrait contains two periodic trajectories—a saddle, and a repellor of spiral type. The inset scroll of the saddle spirals out from the periodic repellor.

The control parameter affects the positions of the inset and outset scrolls of the saddle cycle, without affecting the repellor.

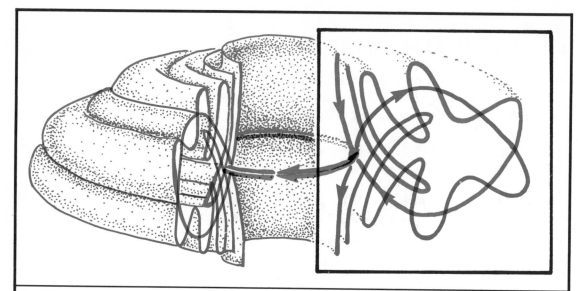

5.3.2. DURING: The homoclinic tangle persists for an interval of control values, not just a single moment of bifurcation. Within this *tangle interval* there is a fractal set of tangency bifurcations, as will be discussed in Section 7.4. Ignoring these details for the present, the periodic repellor persists through it all.

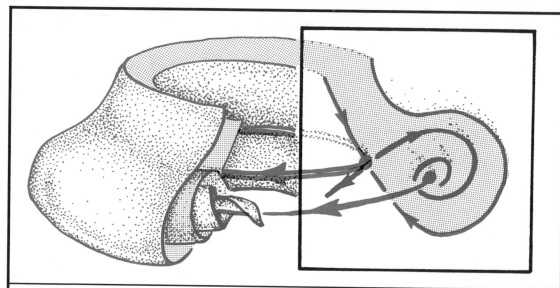

5.3.3. AFTER?: This is the simple *suspension* (prolongation around a cycle) of the impossible Fig. 5.2.4. As the blue outset scroll of the saddle (having passed completely through the green inset scroll as the control parameter moved through the entire tangle interval) rolls up tightly around its limit set, which cannot possibly be the unaffected periodic repellor, there must be a new limit set in the portrait. And there is!

Let's extract the strobe plane for a closer look. Recall that AIT is short for Attractive Invariant Torus.

5.3.4. WELL AFTER! This is the simple suspension of the correct result of the periodic blue sky event, Fig. 5.2.5. The blue outset scroll (shown here in strobe section as a blue curve) wraps up around an AIT, a red torus (seen here in strobe section as a red cycle) engulfing the periodic repellor (appearing in strobe section as a green dot).

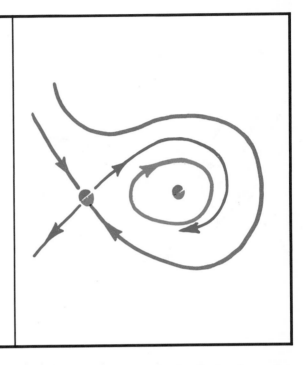

And now, to interpolate some in-betweens, we will run this movie slowly backwards, focusing on the red torus, seen in strobe view.

5.3.5. AFTER. As the control nears the right-hand endpoint of the tangle interval, the section curves of the in-set and outset scrolls approach their first tangency bifurcation, the *off-tangency*. Because a tangency, after one turn around the cycle (or one application of the Poincaré section map), moves onto another tangency, there must be an infinite number of tangencies created simultaneously. Meanwhile, the red torus expands and develops some bulges, as it is pulled toward the tangle by the blue outset.

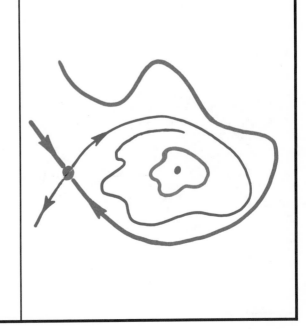

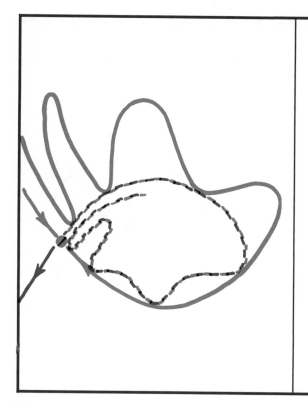

5.3.6. OFF-TANGENCY: Here is the final tangency bifurcation. The inset and outset curves have a one-sided tangle, and the red torus has been pulled into tangency as well, by the infinite sequence of folds of the blue outset.

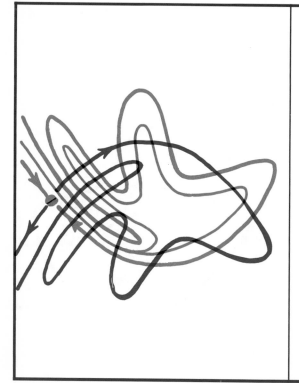

5.3.7. DURING: Within the tangle interval, the red torus becomes a chaotic bagel attractor, as many experiments have shown[1]. There is an infinitude of further tangency bifurcations for control values within this interval.

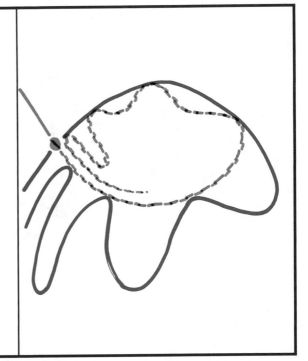

5.3.8. ON-TANGENCY: Now the green inset has been pulled completely through the blue outset, and the first moment of contact has been attained by this reverse sequence. The folds of the red bagel attractor are tangent to the smooth blue inset, in an infinite sequence of points, as well.

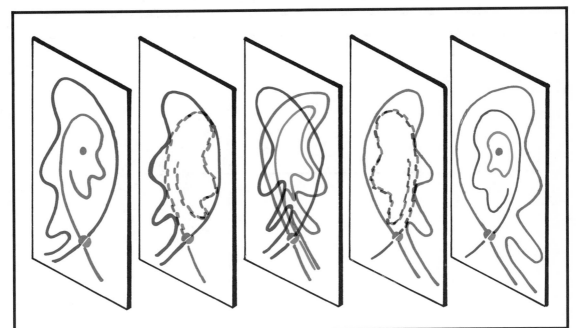

5.3.9. Erecting the strobed portraits in the space of the strobed response diagram, we obtain this side-by-side skeleton. Reading from left to right, we see a chaotic bagel appear out of the blue. This is a catastrophic event involving a chaotic attractor: a *chaotic catastrophe,* or *chaostrophe.*

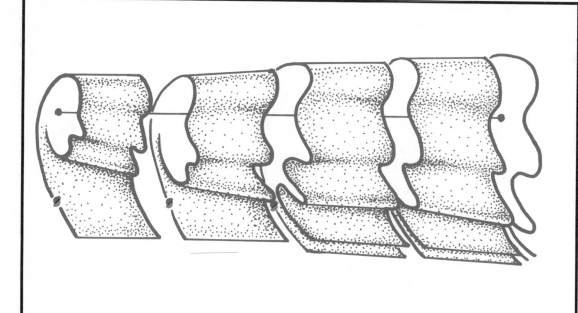

5.3.10. Here we have smoothly interpolated the strobed inset curves, showing their severe folding for control values within the tangle interval.

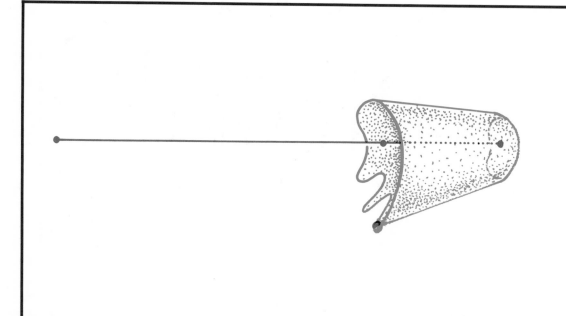

5.3.11. And here, finally, is the cut-away view showing the locus of attraction in the strobed response diagram,

SUMMARY: In this event, an infinitude of microscopic bifurcations within an interval of control values cooperate in the catastrophic creation of a chaotic attractor, which finally settles down to a braid of periodic attractors on an AIT. There are many unanswered questions about this event, which was originally suggested by the suspension construction applied to the periodic blue sky event, and eventually confirmed in experimental work.

5.4 RÖSSLER'S BLUE SKY IN 3D

A similar event, in which a fully developed chaotic attractor disappeared suddenly, was observed by Rössler early in the history of chaotic bifurcations [2]. We start with a Rössler attractor in a 3D flow (see *Part Two,* Section 3.4). In this sequence, it will disappear into the blue.

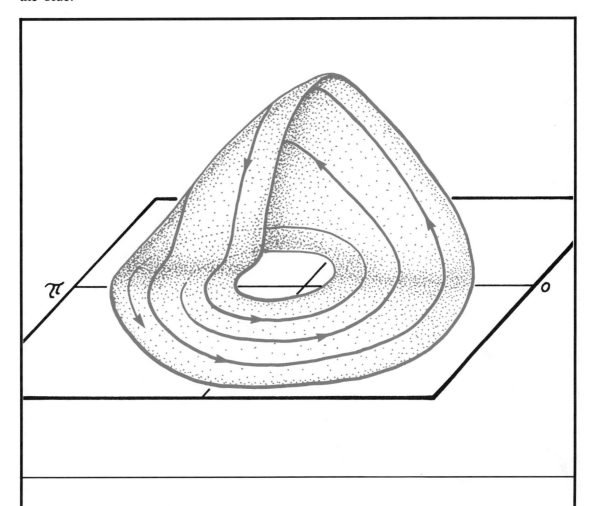

5.4.1. Here is a chaotic attractor which is vaguely periodic. We may cut across it with a strobe section.

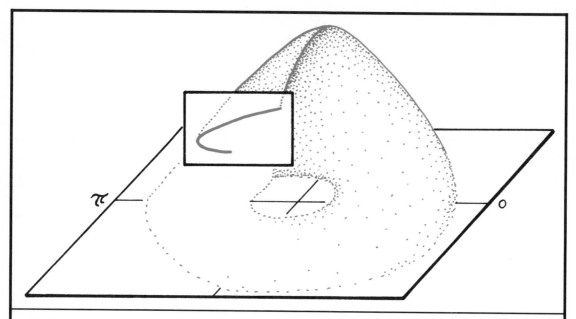

5.4.2. The strobe section reveals the fractal structure of the attractor, and we will describe the blue sky event within this plane.

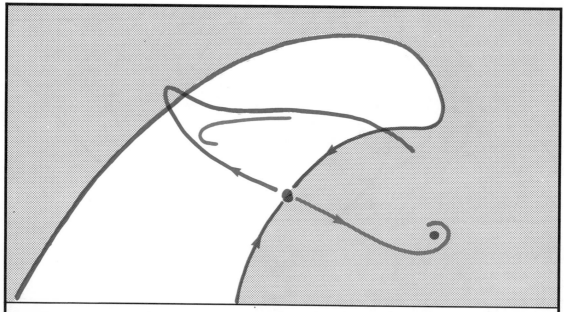

5.4.3. BEFORE: We will start the sequence with this strobe portrait of the Rössler band, nested within the tangle of a nearby homoclinic saddle cycle, as revealed by the computer graphics of Stewart[3]. In the lower left is a periodic attractor, unaffected by the control. The two basins are bounded by the green inset of the periodic saddle.

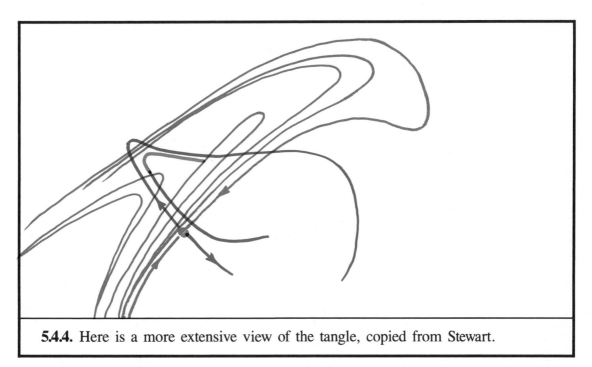

5.4.4. Here is a more extensive view of the tangle, copied from Stewart.

As in the preceding event, the control parameter will affect the crossing of the inset and the outset. This time, we will start with a tangle, and remove the tangle by increasing the control parameter.

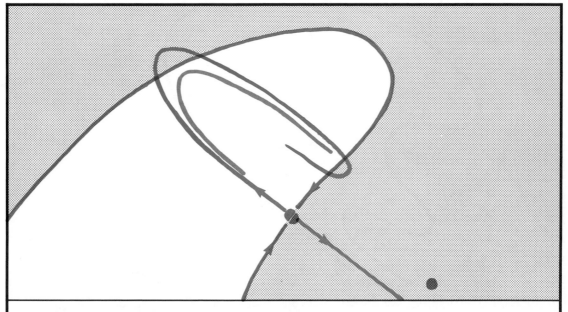

5.4.5. JUST BEFORE: The blue outset is about to pull through the green inset, and the chaotic attractor is close to the blue outset.

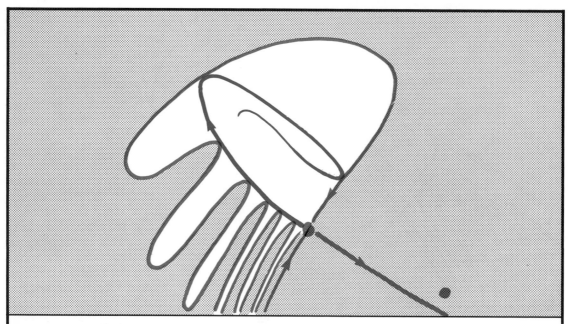

5.4.6. OFF-TANGENCY: At the moment of the last tangency bifurcation, the chaotic attractor is stretched out along one blue loop. Without a microscope, it looks like a band. (See *Part Two,* Fig. 4.4.4 for the micrograph.)

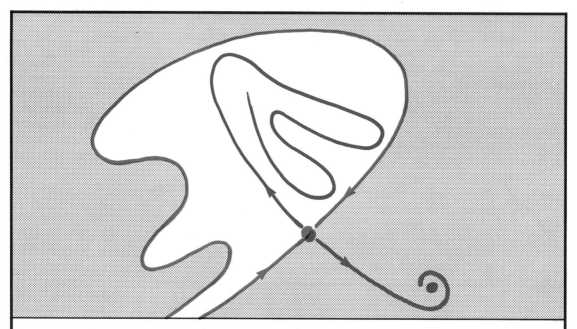

5.4.7. JUST AFTER: Past the last tangency, there is no chaotic attractor. The green inset is now a virtual separatrix, entirely within the blue basin of of the single remaining attractor.

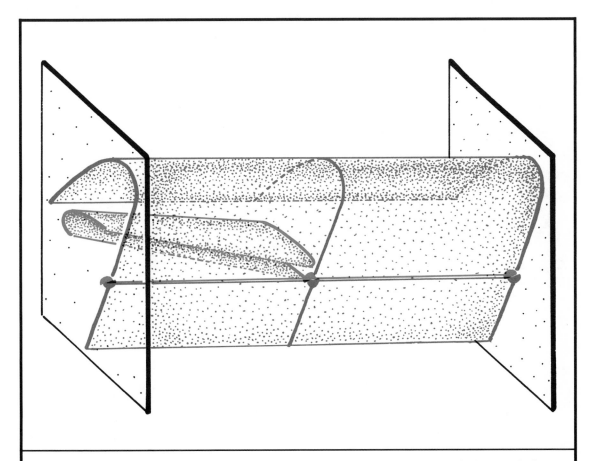

5.4.8. Assembling the strobed portraits in a side-by-side, and smoothly interpolating the loci of attraction and separation, we obtain this response diagram of the Rössler event.

SUMMARY: In this event, frequently observed in digital and analog simulation since the early days of chaotic dynamics, a chaotic band attractor disappears catastrophically into the blue. The involvement of the nearby tangle, fully analysed only recently, is characteristic of many similar events.

6. EXPLOSIVE BIFURCATIONS

After a chapter on subtle bifurcations and three on catastrophes, you may have forgotten that there are three categories of bifurcation: subtle, catastrophic, and explosive. For years we said that there were only two, subtle and catastrophic. It now seems to us that explosions should be regarded as a separate class, rather than being included among the catastrophes. Explosive bifurcations are discontinuous like catastrophes. But like subtle bifurcations, they lack hysteresis. The name and basic concept were given by Smale in 1967 [1]. In any case, here are some simple examples.

6.1. BLUE LOOP IN 2D

There is another way a periodic attractor can pop up, not out of the blue sky, but from a blue loop associated with a saddle point. This example is due to Zeeman [2].

Recall this typical portrait, Fig. 3.2.7, on a sphere. It has critical points, but no limit cycles.

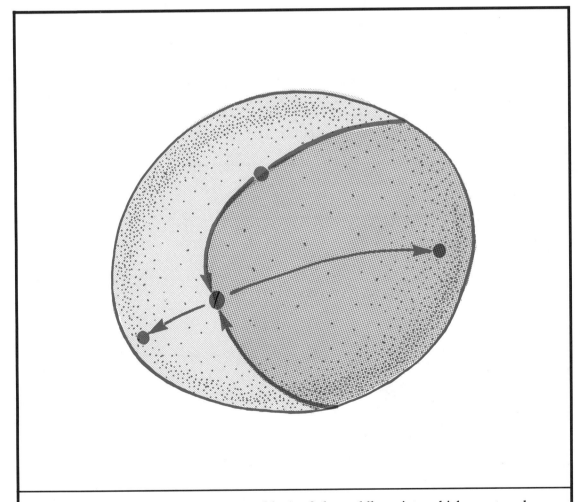

6.1.1. Here, the two outset curves (blue) of the saddle point, which must end up at attractors, belong to *two different* basins. The system is *bistable*. The inset curves (green) actually separate the basins.

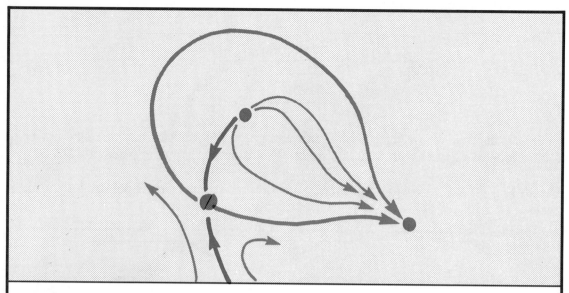

6.1.2. BEFORE: On the other hand, this portrait could arise. Here there is only one attractor and basin. The system is *monostable*. Both outset curves from the saddle point go to the same point attractor. We call this a *blue loop*. The loop encloses a point repellor, and touches a point attractor. The two inset curves of the saddle are virtual separatrices.

Now we will perform a static fold catastrophe (Section 3.2) upon the two critical points of the blue loop.

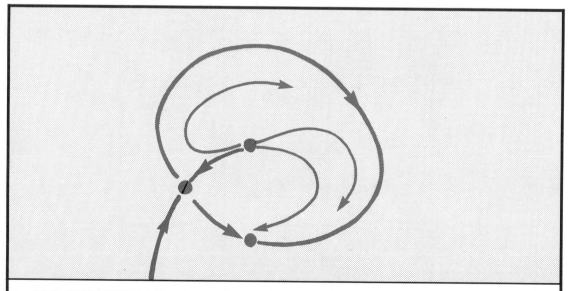

6.1.3. JUST BEFORE: The saddle and attractor points approaching conjunction on one of the outset curves of the saddle. One CE of each is approaching *zero*. The angle made by the two saddle-outset arcs at the point attractor is now 180 degrees.

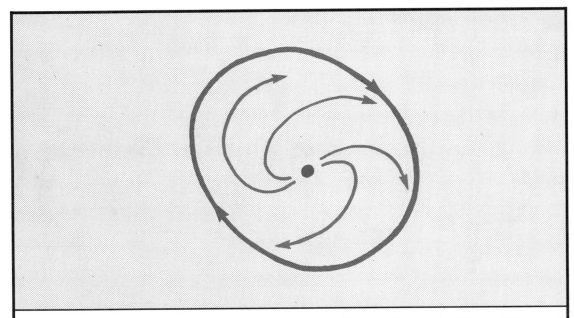

6.1.4. JUST AFTER: The point attractor and the saddle point have mutually annihilated in a static fold catastrophe. *But the blue loop has become a periodic attractor!* The system is still monostable, but the solitary equilibrium state is a slow oscillation with a large amplitude, rather than a rest point.

The point attractor has exploded into a periodic attractor.

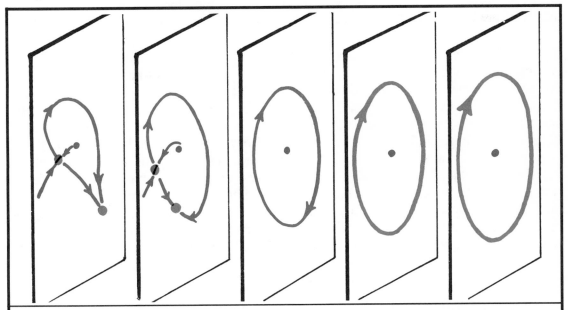

6.1.5. Erecting these phase portraits side-by-side in the control-phase space of the response diagram, we obtain this skeletal representation of the event.

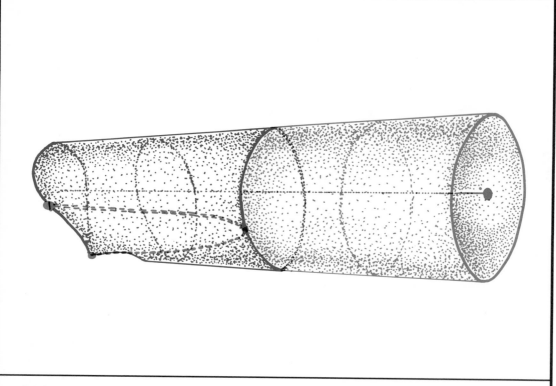

6.1.6. Filling in the continuous red locus of attraction and stripping off some of the green details, we have the response diagram of the blue loop event.

SUMMARY: The static fold catastrophe, in a portrait having a blue loop, results in the explosion of the point attractor into a periodic attractor. The locus of attraction looks like a pot with a handle. The sudden enlargement of an attractor, within its undisturbed basin, is the defining feature of an explosive bifurcation. The event is *reversible* in that the implosion, which takes place as the control is reversed, occurs at the same bifurcation value of the control parameter. The event does not exhibit hysteresis (see *Part One,* Fig. 4.3.7). The *local* event involving the fold is identical to that described in Section 3.2. But the *global* event involving the blue loop makes this event a new entry in our atlas of bifurcations, in which the loci of attraction within the response diagram have top priority. For this reason, the *response diagram* is not exactly identical to the *bifurcation diagram,* as defined by mathematicians. Bifurcation diagrams indicate bifurcation events living entirely within the separatrices, while response diagrams emphasize the bifurcations affecting the loci of attraction only.

6.2. BLUE LOOP IN 3D

The simple suspension, around a cycle, of the preceding event gives rise to a 3D version of essentially the same phenomenon.

Within an unperturbed basin, a periodic attractor may explode into a braided torus (AIT).

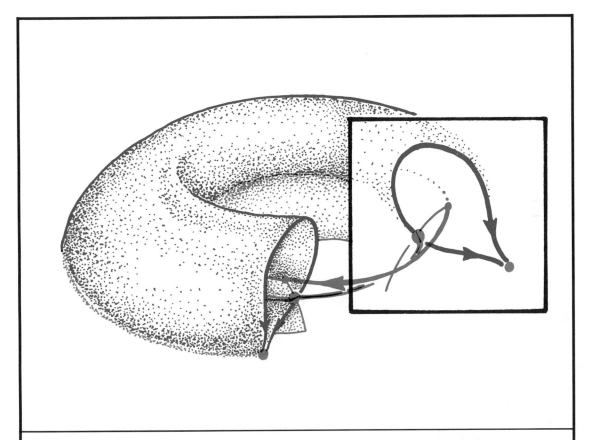

6.2.1. BEFORE: Here is the initial portrait. There are three limit cycles of about the same period going around a ring: attractor, saddle, and repellor. The strobe plane section looks a lot like the initial portrait of the blue loop in 2D. The two leaves of the outset of the saddle (blue surfaces) are both attracted to the same periodic attractor. In strobe section, they form a blue loop. In 3D, they form a blue sleeve, having a crease marked by the periodic attractor (red cycle).

We now increase the control to effect a periodic fold catastrophe, simultaneously annihilating the periodic attractor and saddle.

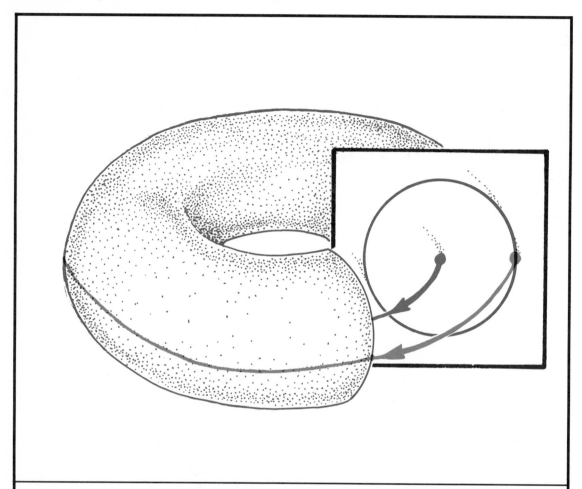

6.2.2. FIRST BIFURCATION: The attractor and saddle are now conjunct, in a nonhyperbolic limit cycle. The crease in the blue sleeve has been ironed out flat. The blue loop in the strobe section is an invariant cycle of the first-return map, having rotation number (average rotation) zero. The *rotation number,* which indicates the number of times that trajectories wind around the waist of the AIT between two flashes of the strobe lamp, is about *zero* throughout this example. But any rational number could have been used. The fluctuating braid bifurcations of a fractal bifurcation event, characteristic of toral dynamics, complicate this event. We postpone discussion of this feature to Section 7.2. For the moment, we just need to know that there is an *interval of fluctuation* in the control range, in which there are an infinite number of bifurcations. These affect only the flow on the torus, and involve minor changes in the number of attractor/saddle cycle pairs braided around the AIT. Some changes in the number of braids may be associated with a change of the rotation number. These involve control intervals of irrational solenoidal flow.

For the present, we may simplify this event by regarding the red AIT as the attractor, throughout the interval of fluctuation. (See Sec. 7.3.).

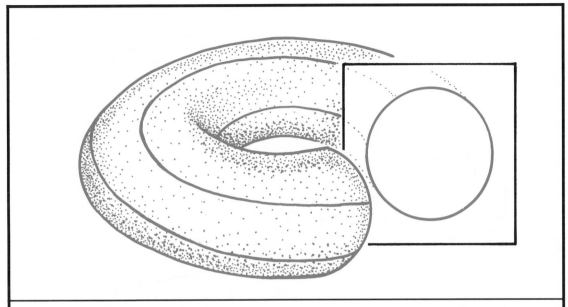

6.2.3. DURING INTERVAL: The blue sleeve has become an attractive invariant torus (AIT), around which trajectories wind only slightly. There are frequent fluctuations in the flow on the torus, betweens braids and solenoids.

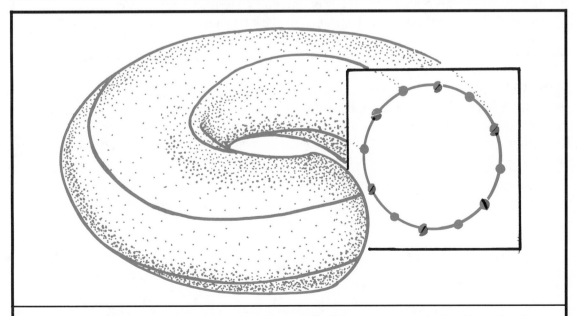

6.2.4. AFTER: The flow on the AIT has settled down to a steady braid, and a few periodic attractors braided on the torus now dominate the portrait.

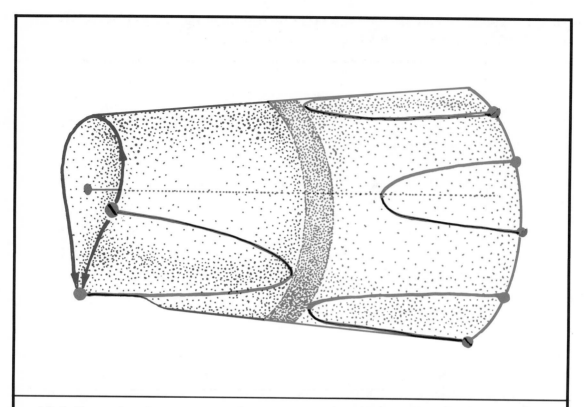

6.2.5. Extracting the strobe planes, erecting them side-by-side in the control-space, and smoothly interpolating the locus of attraction, we obtain this cut-away representation of the strobed response diagram. The dark ring represents the interval of fluctuation.

SUMMARY: In this event, a direct extension of the blue loop in 2D to 3D, a local event (periodic fold catastrophe) is complicated by a global feature (blue sleeve) so that an AIT of large amplitude explodes from the vanishing periodic attractor. When the dust settles, there are several new periodic attractors braided around the former blue sleeve. Many other variants of this explosion are known.

6.3. ZEEMAN'S BLUE TANGLE IN 3D

In the early 1960's, Smale constructed his famous horseshoe example, a 3D flow with a tangled, virtual separatrix (see *Part Three,* Section 5.3). Eventually, chaotic attractors were observed to explode out of periodic attractors associated with such tangles. In this section we develop a version of this event, following Zeeman [3]. Recall the homoclinic tangle, from *Part Three,* Fig. 5.1.9.

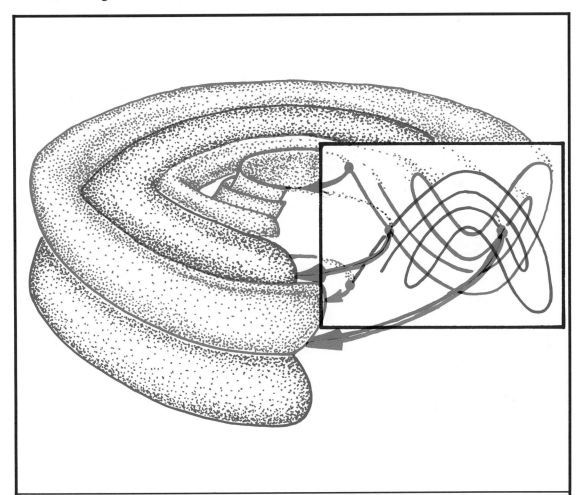

6.3.1. BEFORE: Here we have a global portrait containing four periodic trajectories of about the same period: a repellor, two saddles, and an attractor. (Compare Fig. 6.2.1.) The two saddles are individually homoclinic, and heteroclinic to each other. They are involved in the tangle described by Smale's horseshoe. The global system is monostable, with tangled virtual separatrices within a single basin. The inner saddle (passing through the strobe section on the left) has an untangled inset strip arriving from the repellor, and an untangled outset strip departing for the attractor.

We now increase the control, to effect (locally) a periodic fold catastrophe between the inner saddle and the attractor.

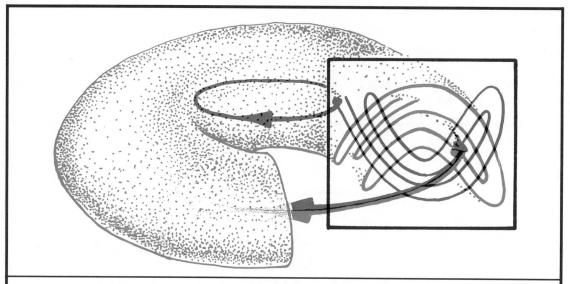

6.3.2. AFTER: The periodic attractor and inner saddle are gone, after mutual annihilation. The remaining saddle is homoclinic as before. But its fractal outset has become the solitary attractor. The global dynamic is still monostable, and the virtual separatrix is only slightly changed.

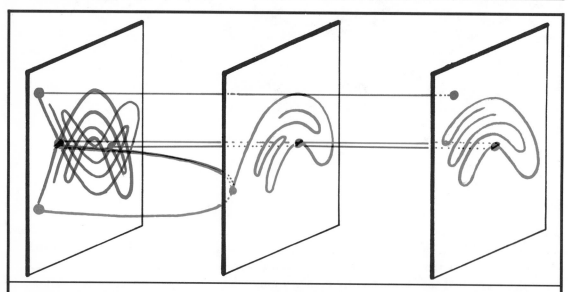

6.3.3. Placing the strobe portraits in their proper places in the space of the strobed response diagram, we interpolate a snapshot of the moment of bifurcation. The inner saddle vanishes along with its blue outset. But the osculating blue outset of the outer saddle turns red.

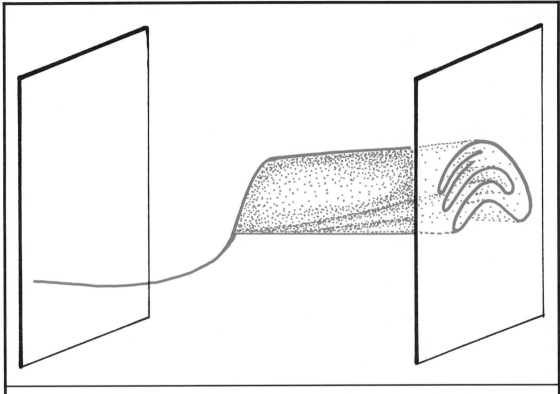

6.3.4. Here is the response diagram, cut away to display the strobed locus of attraction alone.

SUMMARY: In this event, a periodic attractor explodes to a large scale chaotic attractor. This has been suggested by Zeeman as a model for the onset of turbulence. Without a significant change in the basin, an attractor abruptly changes its type, and the volume of the phase space which it dominates.

6.4. UEDA'S CHAOTIC EXPLOSION IN 3D

So far we have seen explosions from point to cycle, from cycle to braid, and from cycle to chaos. It is also possible to have an explosion from small chaos to large chaos. In 1980, this example was published by Ueda [4], the first of the great artists of chaos.

Here, translated to four colors, is an early stage on the way to the Rössler band, from *Part Two,* Fig. 3.4.4. This is obtained from an electronic analog of Duffing's forced pendulum [5].

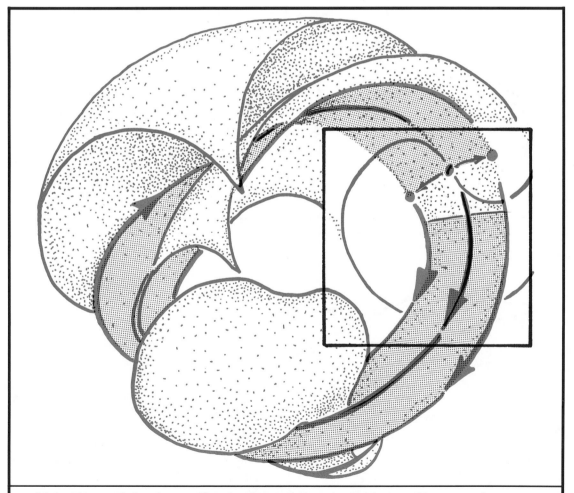

6.4.1. First, we fix the amplitude of the electronic forcing oscillator. Its frequency will be the control knob in this experiment. After a periodic fold catastrophe, a second periodic attractor appears. Here they are, separated by the scrolled green inset of the new periodic saddle. This is a bistable system.

From this point, we will make a few preparatory bifurcations, before beginning the Ueda sequence. These may require changing forcing amplitude as well as frequency, and perhaps other parameters.

We will indicate these preparations in the strobe plane only.

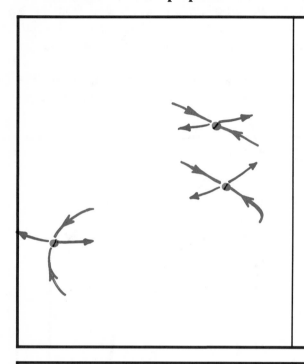

6.4.2. Next, we vary some parameters, and turn these two attractors into saddles. One possibility for accomplishing this would be an octave jump, in which case we imagine the new attractors to have disappeared from view.

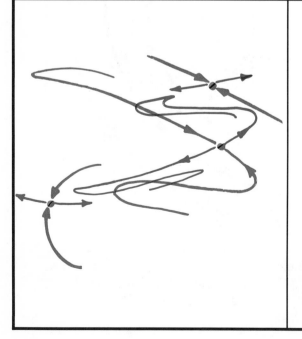

6.4.3. For the next modification, we move the inset and outset of the central saddle, to make two homoclinic tangles. In the window, we show a simplified schematic of the tangles. Note that the loops represent homoclinic tangles (a stable, generic phenomenon), not unstable homoclinic orbits.

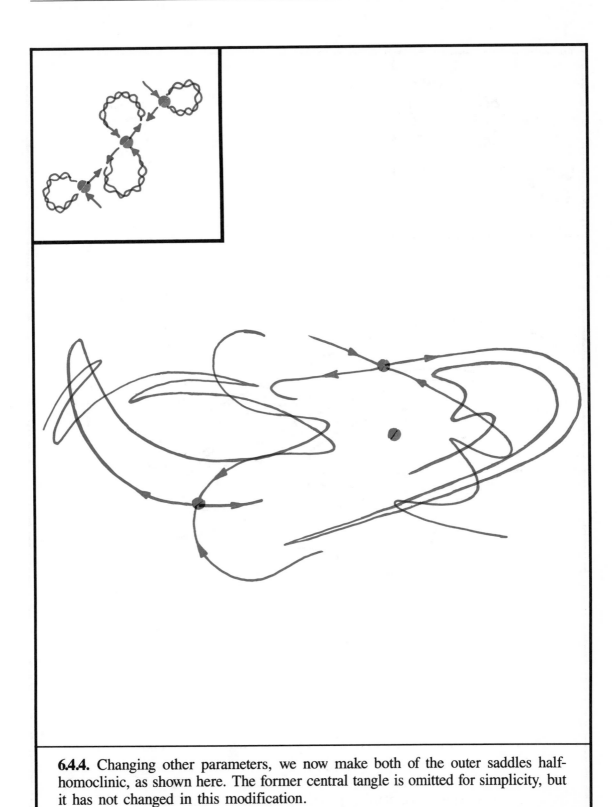

6.4.4. Changing other parameters, we now make both of the outer saddles half-homoclinic, as shown here. The former central tangle is omitted for simplicity, but it has not changed in this modification.

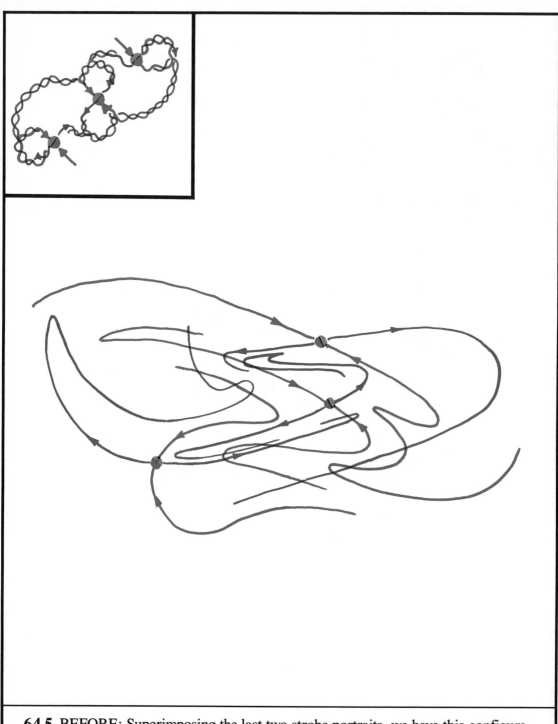

6.4.5. BEFORE: Superimposing the last two strobe portraits, we have this configuration, reproduced from Ueda's computer plot. All tangles are indicated schematically in the window. This is the starting point for our chaotic explosion.

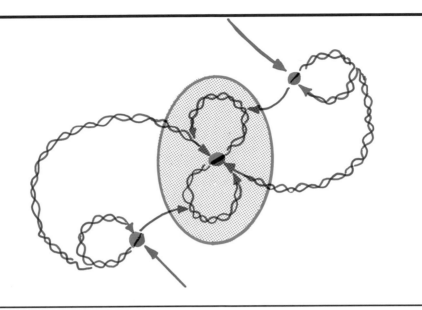

6.4.6. BEFORE: Here is an enlargement of the schematic diagram from the window in the preceding panel. As the outer outsets are attracted to the center tangle, the chaotic attractor in this portrait is the tangled outset of the center saddle. It is contained in the red-shaded region.

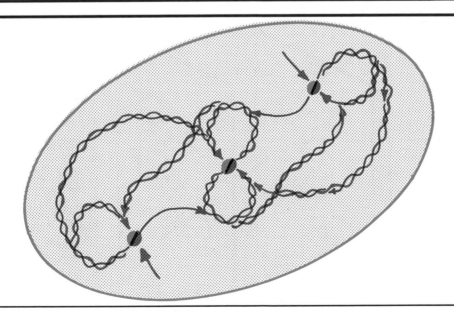

6.4.7. AFTER: The schematic now has new heteroclinic saddle connections, indicated by the bold green arrows here. Now the entire system is tangled, it is a *hypercycle* (see *Part Three*, Section 5.4). The chaotic attractor has exploded so as to include the outsets of the outer saddles.

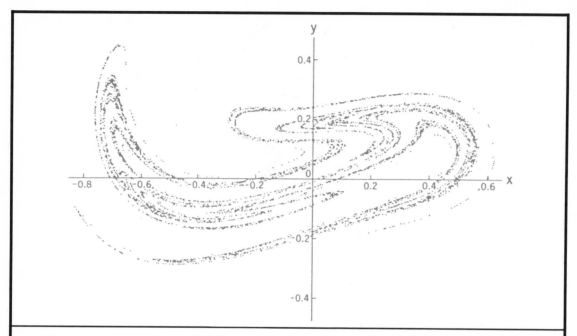

6.4.8. AFTER: Here is the new strobe portrait, corresponding to the new schematic, again reproduced from Ueda.

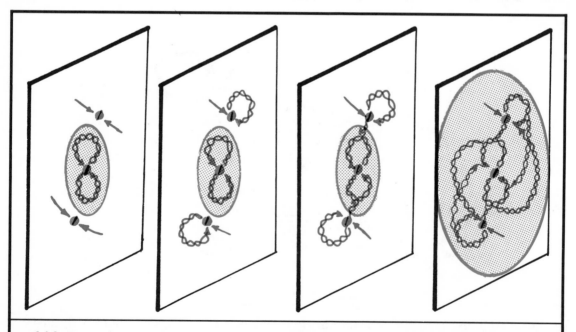

6.4.9. Repeating our usual side-by-side construction in the state/control space of the strobed response diagram, here is the skeleton representation for this chaotic explosion.

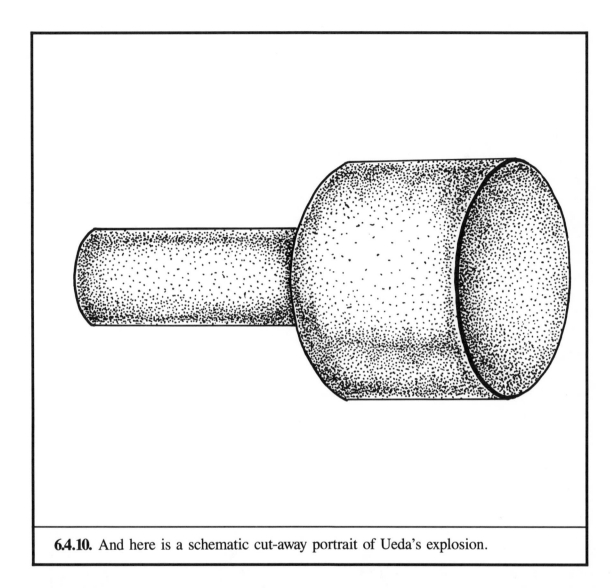

6.4.10. And here is a schematic cut-away portrait of Ueda's explosion.

SUMMARY: In this event, thanks to tangency bifurcations in which structural stability is lost momentarily because of the violation of generic property G3, an attractive tangle is abruptly enlarged through the addition of new foliage to a hypercycle.

7. FRACTAL BIFURCATIONS

Referring to the *big picture,* in which a dynamical scheme is represented as a curve of dynamical systems, we see a bifurcation occurring wherever the curve pierces a hypersurface belonging to the *bad set.* An important feature of the bad set, which we have not illustrated as yet, is the *accumulation* of an infinite number of these bad sheets in fractal systems. Thus, a curve representing a generic scheme may unavoidably encounter an infinite set of bifurcations. Even though such a configuration involves an infinitude of individual bifurcation events, we may regard it as a single atomic bifurcation event. Thus, we speak of *fractal bifurcation events.* In this chapter we illustrate four examples of these fractal events. Many more may occur.

7.1. OCTAVE CASCADE

The simplest fractal bifurcation event is the octave cascade. The infinite set of bifurcation sheets in the big picture are arranged in a simple sequence, like the footprints of the frog jumping halfway to the wall. That is, the sheets get closer and closer to a limit sheet. This configuration is called a *cascade*. Each sheet (individual bifurcation event) in the convergent sequence is the same atomic event: the octave jump in 3D, hence the name, *octave cascade*. (Sometimes this is called the *flip cascade;* see Sec. 2.4). The limit sheet marks the onset of chaotic behavior.

Recall that the Möbius band is fundamental to the octave jump.

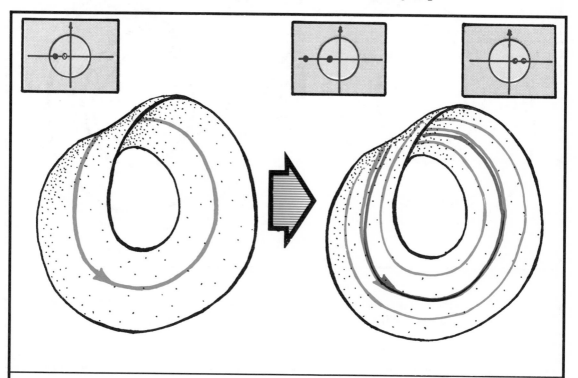

7.1.1. Here is a review of the octave jump in 3D: BEFORE and AFTER. Note that the CMs of the original cycle are both in the left half of the red disk (attractive region of the CM plane) before the event, while one of them (indicating behavior within the twisted band) has moved to the left half of the green (repelling) region after the event. However, the new attractor (corresponding to a tone one octave lower) has one of its CMs on each side of the red disk.

In order to go on with the next step of this cascade, we must adjust the new attractor so that both of its CMs are in the left half of the red disk. This adjustment may be smoothly made if the band is folded in two layers, as indicated in *Part Two,* Section 3.1. And if the band has the folded structure of a Rössler attractor, instead of the twisted structure of a Möbius band, then we may adjust the double period attractor on the band so that it appears to cross itself, but the two branches belong to two different layers of the folded band. The lower branch has been pushed back, over the fold, and down onto the lower sheet. At the same time, the CMs have been pushed to the left of the unit disk.

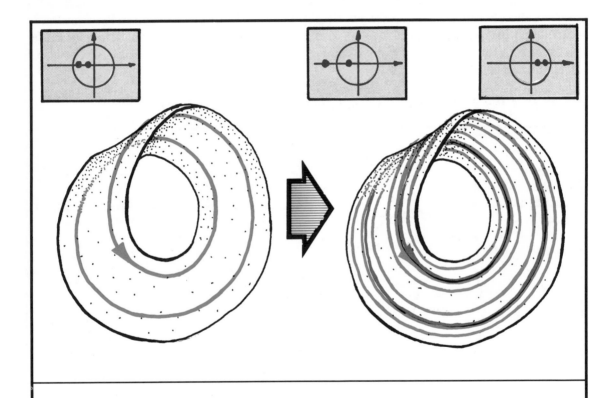

7.1.2. Now we are in a position to repeat the octave jump event. The twice-around attractor becomes a saddle cycle, and a four-times-around attractor takes over the basin.

To continue these events in a infinite cascade, we need more and more layers of the folded band, as are found in the Rössler attractor. And after each octave jump, we need another fold of the underlying band, to adjust the CMs to the left half of the unit disk, in preparation for another jump. Indeed, after the convergence of the cascade of individual octave jumps, we find the attractor has become a chaotic band.

This is one of the first chaotic scenarios to be discovered experimentally, by Rössler in 1971 [1].

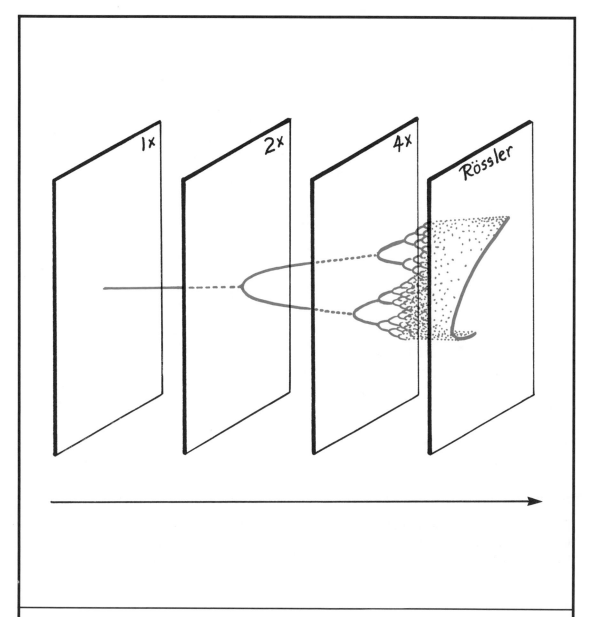

7.1.3. Here, then, is the strobed response diagram of the octave cascade. Each vertical plane corresponds to a strobe plane section through the infinitely-folded band. Each octave jump is represented by a fork as explained in Fig. 2.4.5. These accumulate in an infinite sequence of multiplications, and converge on a chaotic band. The bifurcation set in the control interval is fractal, (see *Part Two,* Sec. 4.4) and the chaotic attractor at the end of the event is fractal as well.

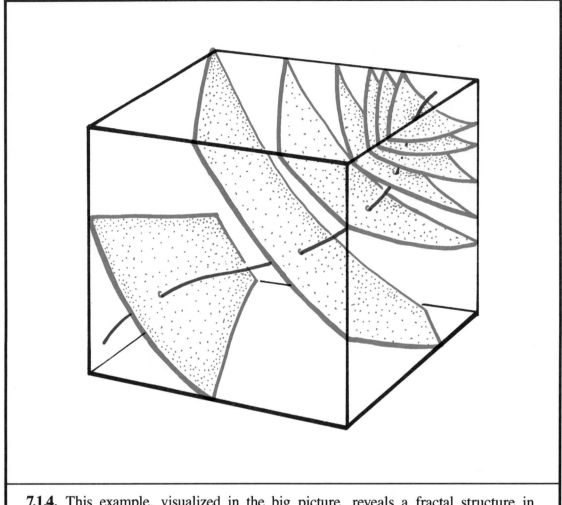

7.1.4. This example, visualized in the big picture, reveals a fractal structure in superspace.

SUMMARY: In this fractal bifurcation event, an infinite number of successive octave jumps accumulate on a phantom Rössler band, which eventually becomes the attractor.
NOTE: We have used *fractal* loosely here, as the dimension of the bifurcation set is actually zero.

7.2. NOISY CASCADE

This event may be viewed as a simple modification of the preceding one. First, regard the Rössler attractor as a noisy oscillator, as suggested in *Part Two,* Section 4.5. Then, replace each oscillator in the octave cascade by a noisy oscillator.

An individual bifurcation which has not been presented earlier in our atlas is the principal actor in the scenario: the chaotic octave jump.

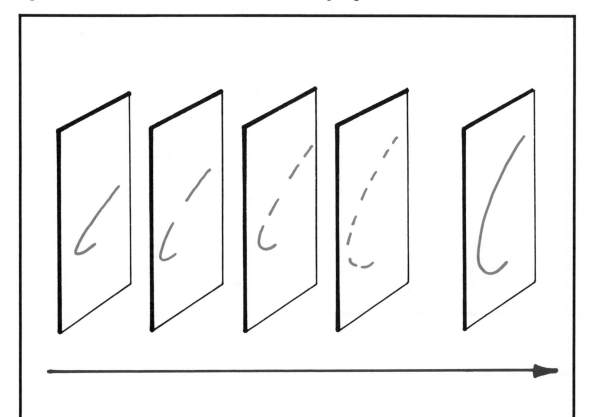

7.2.1. Here is a side-by-side skeleton of the strobed response diagram, showing the entire cascade. From left to right, a Rössler attractor makes an octave jump, turning into a twice-around band, shown here in strobe plane section. This is repeated in a convergent sequence, but at the limiting end, the final configuration on the right is again a once-around band!

In actuality, this cascade occurs on the other side of the limit attained by the octave jump for periodic attractors, as discovered by Lorenz [2].

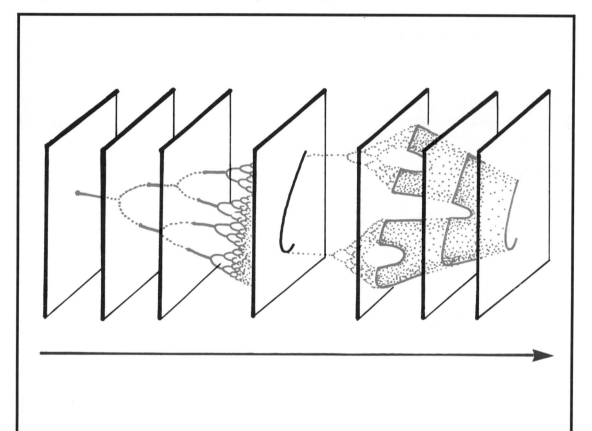

7.2.2. Here is a stripped-down view of the strobed response diagram for the full event, showing a periodic cascade approaching from the left, and a noisy one from the right.

SUMMARY: In this event, the bifurcation set in the control interval consists of two convergent sequences, approaching the same limit point from opposite sides. A generic scheme, as a curve in the big picture, might encounter a doubly infinite set of sheets of the bad set. Unavoidably, this bifurcation event would result.

7.3. BRAID BIFURCATIONS

We have referred repeatedly to rearrangements of the braided periodic attractors encountered in toral dynamics *(Part One,* Chapter 5, and *Part Two,* Section 3.2). We now review this phenomenon in the Big Picture.

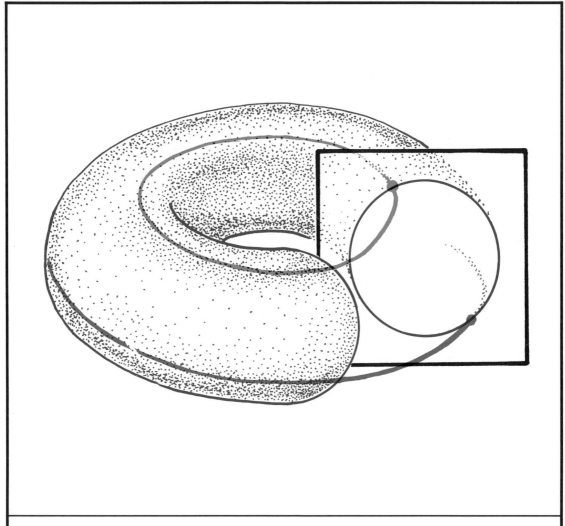

7.3.1. We might begin with the simplest toral flow, with two periodic trajectories: an attractor and a repellor. The rotation number (average rotation of the Poincaré first-return map on the strobe section) in this case is *zero*.

Alternatively, the rotation number could be any number of full circles, if the two periodic trajectories wound around the waist of the torus a few times before the first return to the strobe plane. In fact, any rational number may arise as a rotation number in this context. On the other hand, there could be any number of periodic attractors, interspersed with an equal number of periodic repellors on the torus. In this case, the rotation number may still be zero.

However, we now consider the simple case pictured, and ask: what happens if the control parameter changes the rotation number?

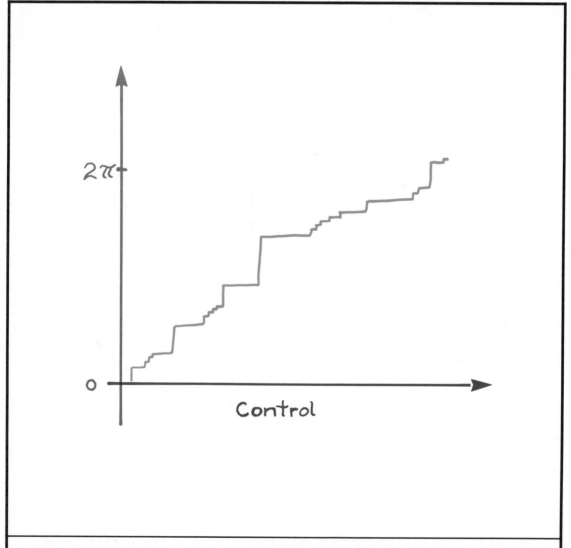

7.3.2. The answer is: this *devil's staircase.* As the control parameter increases to the right in this fictitious example, the rotation number increases from zero to one full revolution, but not smoothly.

But there are an infinite number of rational numbers in this rotation interval. And at each and every one of them, the rotation number tends to dwell awhile, in spite of the still increasing control parameter. This is because toral flows with rational rotations typically are structurally stable (according to Peixoto's theorem, *Part Three,* Section 3.2) with a stable braid of periodic attractors and repellors which wind appropriately. The irrational rotations, less likely, always correspond to solenoidal flows *(Three,* Fig. 1.3.13). These may still fill up a set of control parameters having substantial expectation (probability larger than zero). This situation is known as a *fat fractal* bifurcation set. The bifurcation set in the control interval is a Cantor set, or fractal, as there are infinite sequences of control values of solenoidal flows (structurally unstable, hence bifurcations, the risers of the staircase) converging to an infinity of control values at the endpoints of control intervals (the steps of the staircase) corresponding to a stable rational braid. This has been beautifully analyzed by Michel [3].

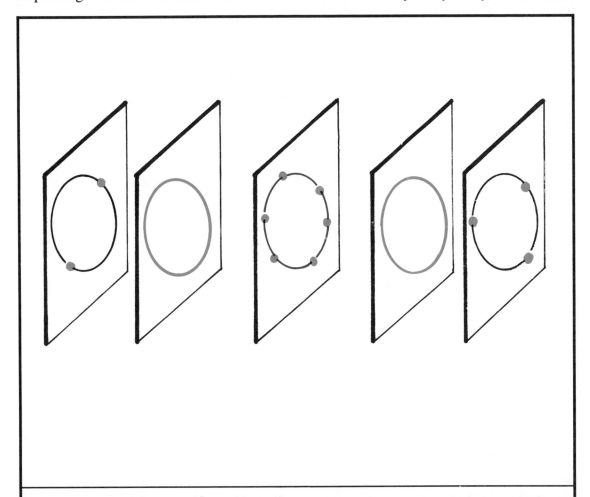

7.3.3. Here are the side-by-side strobe planes for this scheme. The red cycles indicate ephemeral solenoidal flows, while the blue cycles with red and green dots signify the stable braids with rational rotations, which survive for a small interval of control parameter values.

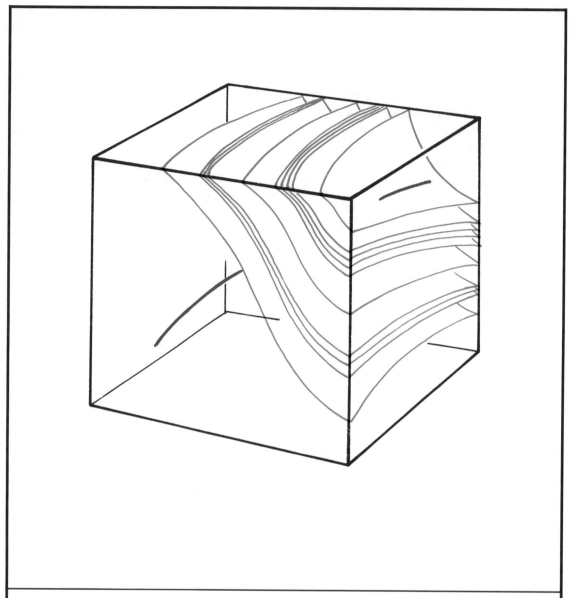

7.3.4. And here is the big picture, showing a thick slice of superspace in which the fractal sheets of braid bifurcations accumulate.

SUMMARY: All AIT's in a dynamical scheme are troubled by the fluctuating braid bifurcations. Thus, it is pragmatic in many applications to regard an attractive torus as a kind of generalized attractor, and ignore as far as possible the microscopic details of its internal dynamic. As in all the bifurcation events in this chapter, we usually regard the entire fractal set of bifurcations as a single bifurcation event. These are characterized by a *bifurcation interval* enclosing the fractal bifurcation set, rather than a single bifurcation point in the control space.

7.4. TANGLE BIFURCATIONS

We have seen, in Chapter 5, that saddle connection bifurcations in 3D or more involve tangles. In the blue bagel, for example, as the control parameter increases and the affected inset and outset strips approach each other, there is a bifurcation point of first contact. The two invariant strips have an infinity of tangencies, which are nongeneric (failing G3) and thus structurally unstable: bifurcations. Later, there was a final bifurcation of tangency, before the two strips have completely passed through one another. These two extreme values define an interval, which we have called the *tangle interval*. For an infinite number of control values (belonging to a fractal set) within the tangle interval, other tangencies may be expected. At these bifurcations, the *signature* of the tangle changes. (See *Part Three,* Section 4.5). Thus, tangles imply an interval of control values which are dominated by a fractal bifurcation set, and which may be regarded as a single bifurcation event. These events have been extensively studied by Newhouse and others [4].

CONCLUSION

In early 1980, we returned to Santa Cruz from different journeys. Full of enthusiasm, we undertook this project. Now, eight years, 740 pages, and 850 figures later, we rest our case, and our bones. This volume, an atlas of bifurcations with one control parameter, has been our main goal throughout. The earlier books have been planned to provide the minimum background necessary for this one. When our energies are replenished by further travels, we may resume our joint work with more vismath books on some of the important subjects we have had to omit so far, such as: ergodic theory, bifurcations with two controls, and of course, manifolds and mappings.

NOTES

Chapter One
[1] See Jones for a thrilling history.
[2] See Todhunter, esp. Chs. 1–13.
[3] See Anon.
[4] See Hagihara, especially the Introduction; and Chandrasekar, Introduction.
[5] See Lyttleton, esp. Chs. 1, 2.
[6] Todhunter, p.181.
[7] Todhunter, p. 208.
[8] Lyttleton, p. 39.
[9] Lyttleton, p. 40.
[10] Lyttleton, p. 45.
[11] Lyttleton, p. 41; Hagihara, p. 2.
[12] Lyttleton, pp. 1–5.
[13] For a very compact review of this crucial paper, see Gurel.
[14] See, for example, Iooss and Joseph.
[15] Abraham, Marsden, and Ratiu, Ch. 8.
[16] Donnely. See also, Coles.
[17] Thom, 1972, 1975, 1983.

Chapter Two
[1] Thom.
[2] See, for example, Prigogine.
[3] Marsden and McCracken.
[4] Hassard, Kazarninoff and Wan.
[5] Hirsch and Smale is one of the best for this purpose.

Chapter Three
[1] See Thom, Zeeman, Poston and Stewart.
[2] Besides the above, see Postle.

Chapter Five
[1] See Abraham and Scott, Abraham and Simo, Abraham and Stewart, and Thompson and Stewart, p. 282.
[2] Rössler, 1976; Simo, 1979; Thompson and Stewart, pp. 280–284.
[3] Stewart, Fig. 6; Thompson and Stewart, p. 282.

Chapter Six
[1] See Smale.
[2] Zeeman, 1982; Thompson and Stewart, p. 130.
[3] Zeeman, 1982; Thompson and Stewart, p. 143.
[4] Ueda, 1980; Simo, 1979; Thompson and Stewart, pp. 234, 278.
[5] Actually, this preceded Duffing. See Martienssen.

Chapter Seven
[1] Rössler, 1976; Thompson and Stewart, p. 242.
[2] Lorenz, 1980.
[3] See, for example, Herman.
[4] Newhouse, also, Guckenheimer and Holmes, p. 331.

BIBLIOGRAPHY

*denotes a book
**denotes a basic text of bifurcation theory

*Abraham, Ralph H., Jerrold E. Marsden, and Tudor Ratiu, *Manifolds, Tensor Analysis, and Applications,* Addison-Wesley, Reading, MA, 1983.

Abraham, Ralph H., and Katherine A. Scott, Chaostrophes of forced Van der Pol systems; in: *Chaos, Fractals, and Dynamics,* (P. Fisher, W. Smith, eds.), M. Dekker, New York, 1985; pp. 123–134.

Abraham, Ralph H., and Carles Simo, Bifurcations and chaos in forced Van der Pol systems, in: *Dynamical Systems and Singularities,* (S. Pnevmatikos, ed.), North-Holland, Amsterdam, 1986; pp. 313–323.

Abraham, Ralph H., and H. Bruce Stewart, A chaotic blue sky catastrophe in forced relaxation oscillations, *Physica 21D,* 1986, pp. 394–400.

Anon., Maupertuis and the flattening of the Earth, *Geographical Journal* 98 (1941), pp. 291–293.

*Chandrasekar, S., *Ellipsoidal Figures of Equilibrium,* Yale University Press, New Haven, CT, 1969.

Coles, C., Transition in circular Couette flow, *J. Fluid Mech.* 21 (1965), pp. 385–425.

Donnelly, R. J., et al, *Phys. Rev. Lett.* 44 (1980), p. 987.

**Guckenheimer, John and Philip Holmes, *Nonlinear Oscillations, Dynamical Systems, and Bifurcations of Vector Fields,* Springer-Verlag, New York, 1983.

Gurel, Okan, Poincaré's bifurcation analysis, *Ann. N. Y. Acad. Sci.* 316 (1979), pp. 5–22.

*Hagihara, Yusuke, *Theories of Equilibrium Figures of a Rotating Homogeneous Fluid Mass,* NASA, Washington, DC, 1935, 1970.

*Hassard, B. D., N. D. Kazarninoff, and Y.H. Wan, *Theory and Applications of Hopf Bifurcation,* Cambridge University Press, Cambridge, 1981.

*Herman, Michael Robert, Sur la conjugaison differentiable des diffeomorphismes du cercle a des rotations, *Institute des Hautes Etudes, Publ. Math.* 49, (1979) 5–234.

*Hirsch, Morris W., and Stephen Smale, *Differential Equations, Dynamical Systems, and Linear Algebra,* Academic Press, New York, 1974.

**Iooss, G., *Bifurcations of Maps and Applications,* North-Holland, Amsterdam, 1979.

*Iooss, Gerard, and Daniel D. Joseph, *Elementary Stability and Bifurcation Theory,* Springer-Verlag, New York, 1980.

James, Preston E., and Goethey, J.M., *All Possible Worlds: A History of Geographical Ideas* (2nd ed.), Wiley, New York, 1972, 1981.

*Jones, Tom B., *The Figure of the Earth,* Coronado Press, Lawrence, KS, 1967.

Leroi-Gourhan, André, *Treasures of Prehistoric Art,* Abrams, New York, 1967.

Lorenz, E. N., Noisy periodicity and reverse bifurcation, in: *Nonlinear Dynamics,* (R. H. G. Helleman, ed.), N. Y. Acad. Sci., New York, 1980.

*Lyttleton, R. A., *The Stability of Rotating Liquid Masses,* Cambridge University Press, Cambridge, 1953.

Marsden, Jerrold E., and Marjorie McCracken, *The Hopf Bifurcation and its Applications,* Springer-Verlag, New York, 1976.

Martienssen, O., Uber neue Resonanzerscheinungen in Wechselstromkreisen, *Physikalische Zeitschrit,* 11 (1910), 448–460.

Newhouse, Sheldon. E., The abundance of wild hyperbolic sets and non-smooth stable sets for diffeomorphisms, *IHES Publ. Math.* 50 (1979), pp. 101–152.

*Postle, Denis, *Catastrophe Theory,* Fontana, London, 1980.

**Poston, Tim, and Ian Stewart, *Catastrophe Theory and its Applications,* Pitman, London, 1978.

*Prigogine, Ilya, *From Being to Becoming: Time and Complexity in the Physical Sciences,* Freeman, San Francisco, CA, 1980.

Rössler, Otto, Different types of chaos in two simple differential equations, *Z. Naturforsch.* 31a (1976), pp. 1664–1670; esp. p. 1668.

Simo, Carles, On the Henon-Pomeau attractor, *J. Stat. Phys.,* 21 (1979), pp. 465–494. 1979

Smale, Stephen, Differential dynamical systems, *Bull. Am. Math. Soc.* 73 (1967), 747–817.

Stewart, H. Bruce, A new form of catastrophe in forced anharmonic oscillators, preprint, Fig. 6.

**Thom, Rene, *Stabilite Structurelle et Morphogenese: essai d'une theorie generale des models,* Benjamin, Reading, MA, 1972.

**Thom, Rene, *Structural Stability and Morphogenesis,* Benjamin-Cummings, Menlo Park, CA, 1975.

**Thom, Rene, *Mathematical Models of Morphogenesis,* Horwood, Chichester, 1983.

**Thompson, J. M. T., and H. B. Stewart, *Nonlinear Dynamics and Chaos,* Wiley, New York, 1986.

*Todhunter, I., *A History of the Mathematical Theories of Attraction and the Figure of the Earth: From the Time of Newton to that of Laplace,* Dover, New York, 1873, 1962.

Ueda, Yoshi, Explosion of strange attractors exhibited by Duffing's equation, in: *Nonlinear Dynamics* (R. H. G. Helleman, ed.), N. Y. Acad. Sci., New York, 1981, pp. 422–434.

**Zeeman, E. Christopher, *Catastrophe Theory: Selected Papers, 1972–1977.* Addison-Wesley, Reading, MA, 1977.

Zeeman, E. Christopher, Bifurcation, catastrophe, and turbulence, in: *New Directions in Applied Mathematics,* (Peter J. Hilton and Gail S. Young, eds.), Springer-Verlag, New York, 1982.

INDEX

Also Available in the Dynamics Series:

Part One: Periodic Behavior   *4-color, 220 pages, 342 illustrations*

Periodic Behavior develops the simple limit sets — *static equilibrium point and periodic limit cycle* — in historical context, and with numerous illustrated examples. The forced pendulum of Duffing and the forced oscillator of Van der Pol are treated extensively. These basic concepts and examples are basic to the following volumes.

Part One chapters include the following:
• Basic Concepts of Dynamics
• Classical Applications: Limit point in 2D from Newton to Rayleigh
• Vibrations: Limit cycles in 2D from Rayleigh to Rashevsky
• Forced Vibrations: Limit cycles in 3D from Rayleigh to Duffing
• Compound Oscillations: Invariant Tori in 3D from Huyghens to Hayashi

Part Two: Chaotic Behavior   *2-color, 137 pages, 170 illustrations*

Chaotic Behavior completes the local theory of dynamical systems by describing the *chaotic limit sets and attractors* of theory and experiment. The examples of Poincaré, Birkhoff, Lorenz and Rössler are described in detail. The chaotic aspects of these examples — unpredictability, sensitive dependence on initial conditions, information gain and noisy power spectra — are fully explained.

Part Two chapters include the following:
• Static Limit Sets and Characteristic Exponents
• Periodic Limit Sets and Characteristic Multipliers
• Chaotic Limit Sets
• Attributes of Chaos

Part Three: Global Behavior   *2-color, 123 pages, 136 illustrations*

Global Behavior develops the full, global portrait of a dynamical system — emphasizing its *multiple attractors, basins, and separatrices*. Generic properties, structural stability, and the fractal microstructure of tangled separatrices are painstakingly treated. All kinds of tangled insets and outsets (of heterclinic saddle points and cycles) are shown in exceptional detail. The revolutionary development of mathematical dynamics, in the 1960's, are presented.

Part Three chapters include the following:
• Global Phase Portraits
• Generic Properties
• Structural Stability
• Heteroclinic Tangles
• Nontrivial Recurrence

Disk One: Periodic Attractors in the Plane

Disk Two: Chaotic Attractors in 3D

These two disks illustrate the exemplary systems from *Part One: Periodic Behavior* and *Part Two: Chaotic Behavior,* with interactive computer graphic programs in compiled BASIC for the Apple II and IBM PC computers. (MS-DOS, 2.0) Please specify Apple or IBM disks when placing an order.

Science Frontier Express Series

Volume One: The Dripping Faucet as a Model Chaotic System *by Robert Shaw*

One of the most exciting recent developments in dynamical system theory has been the emergence of a better understanding of the **"chaotic transition,"** the change of behavior of many systems from periodic to nonperiodic behavior. In this work, the author shows that the pattern of drops from a simple faucet makes such a transition, as the tap is slowly opened. This physical example is used to address the important general question: if a system is chaotic, how chaotic is it?

Information theory, the author argues, provides the appropriate tools for sorting out mixtures of determinism and chaos. Although this work describes the very latest results in the application of information theory to dynamical systems, the presentation is as nontechnical as possible. The text is illustrated by more than 60 pictures, and every effort has been made to make the material accessible to a wide audience. The result is a remarkably clear discussion of the concepts of "entropy" and "information" in the context of dynamical systems — easily readable, for example, by students of Shannon's book on information theory. The book ends on a more philosophical note, with a personal view of the issues which will loom largest in the future development of the subject.

lll pages, 63 illustrations

Volume Two: On Morphodynamics *by Ralph Abraham*

On Morphodyanmics includes selected papers written by Dr. Ralph Abraham on models for pattern formation processes, morphogenesis, and self-organizing systems, showing the evolution of the **complex dynamical systems** concept over a fifteen-year period. The works indicate a range of applications spanning the physical, biological, and social sciences.

The volume includes:

1. *Stability of models,* 50 pages, 1967.

2. *Introduction to morphology,* 126 pages, 1972.

3. *Psychotronic vibrations,* 4 pages, 1973.

4. *Vibrations and the realization of form,* 18 pages, 1976.

5. *The macroscopy of resonance,* 8 pages, 1976.

6. *Simulation of cascades by videofeedback,* 5 pages, 1976.

7. *The function of mathematics in the evolution of the noosphere,* 15 pages, 1980.

8. *Dynamics and self-organization,* 28 pages, 1980.

9. *Dynamical models for thought,* 22 pages, 1981.

225 pages, 55 illustrations

Vismath Videos

Mathematics Into Pictures   *Dr. E. C. Zeeman*

Six 50-minute lectures, 1978 series given by invitation of the BBC. Royal Institution Christmas Lectures. (Guild Sound and Vision). Video: VHS or Umatic formats.

Space-Time Dynamics in Video Feedback and
Chaotic Attractors of Driven Oscillators   *J. P. Crutchfield*

Demonstrates pattern formation, self-organization, and phase transitions in video feedback. Investigates geometric structure of chaotic attractors. Narration and music track included, 29 minutes. Video: VHS, Umatic, or Beta formats.

Studying Artificial Life with Cellular Automata   *C. G. Langton*

Illustrates attempts to bring about the "living state" in a logical universe called a cellular automation. 23 minutes. Video: VHS or U-matic formats.

Vismath Films

The Lorenz System   *Bruce Stewart*

The first in a series of high resolution computer animated movies on nonlinear dynamics, *The Lorenz System* shows a visual example of elementary chaos. Edward Lorenz's model of thermally driven convection is explained in a standard 16mm color film of 25 minutes duration. Because the subject matter itself is three-dimensional and dynamic, the film format can bring fundamental ideas from the research frontier within the reach of non-specialists.

The film introduces the fluid dynamical model leading to the dynamical system, and constructs phase portraits of the system for a wide range of parameter values. Ideas are introduced step by step, beginning with the notion of phase space itself. The presentation is entirely visual, without equations, but with frequent captions explaining the important ideas. The major bifurcations in the Lorenz system are seen, and the manifold outstructure emanating from the equilibria is examined in the laminar, pre-chaotic, and chaotic regimes. The geometry of period doubling cascades is observed.

The Lorenz System is suitable for college-level students of differential equations, fluid mechanics, or nonlinear oscillations. Anyone who deals with nonlinear models of dynamics (in physics, chemistry, biology, ecology) can gain valuable insight from the film.   *Film: 25 minutes, color, 16mm*

Strange Attractor in a Chemical System   *Robert Shaw, Jean-Claude Roux & Harry Swinney*

Experimental data from a stirred chemical reactor, plotted according to the graphical scheme of nonlinear dynamics, reveals a geometric figure essentially identical to the famous Rössler attractor of chaotic dynamics. (Section 3.4 of *Part Two, Dynamics: The Geometry of Behavior*). This film shows the experiment, the graphical scheme, and the structure of the reactor, in exquisite detail, using state-of-the-art equipment. A brief written description accompanies the movie.

Film: 20 minutes, black & white, 16mm

Chaotic Attractors of Driven Oscillators   *J. P. Crutchfield*

This movie studies a series of classic nonlinear oscillators. The technique used is that of animated Poincaré sections. This is the temporal animation of cross sections through an attractor. A single Poincaré section is made by collecting the oscillator's position and velocity at a fixed phase of the driving force. The animation then plays back in time successive sections as the driving phase advances. The technique allows one to easily see and study the folding and stretching geometry around the attractors.

The movie presents five chaotic attractors taken from three different nonlinear oscillators. The first three examples come from Shaw's variant of the driven Van der Pol oscillator. (See Sec. 3.2 of *Part Two, Dynamics: The Geometry of Behavior.*) The first exhibits the folding action of three "ears" on a torus attractor. The second "ribbon" attractor is the consequence of a period-doubling route to chaos. The final Van der Pol example reveals a complex attractor with visible fractal leaves. The movie illustrates the first attractor's symmetries by superimposing sections.

The fourth attractor comes from Duffing's oscillator. (See Chapter 4, *Part One, Dynamics: The Geometry of Behavior.*) Within its thick fractal structure, it is reminiscent of oriental brush-stroked characters. The final example is the driven damped pendulum. As the attractor is spatially period and of infinite extent, a "five-well" segment is shown. With the animation it appears as a train of ocean waves continually breaking on a beach.

The movie *Chaotic Attractors if Driven Oscillators* was filmed during the fall of 1981 and premiered at Dynamics Day, La Jolla, California. A brief written description accompanies the movie.

Film: 12 minutes, black & white, 16mm

Order Form

Aerial Press, Inc., P.O. Box 1360, Santa Cruz, CA 95061
(408) 425-8619

QTY.	ITEM	PRICE	Shipping Cost Per Item			TOTALS *(add shipping)*
			U.S.	Canada	All Others	
	Dynamics: Part I (Abraham & Shaw)	$34.00	$3.00	$6.00	$10.00	
	Dynamics: Part II (Abraham & Shaw)	$28.00	$3.00	$6.00	$10.00	
	Dynamics: Part III (Abraham & Shaw)	$28.00	$3.00	$6.00	$10.00	
	Dynamics: Part IV (Abraham & Shaw)	$38.00	$3.00	$6.00	$10.00	
	Disk I (IBM-PC or Apple II)	$25.00	$2.00	$4.00	$6.00	
	Disk II (IBM-PC or Apple II)	$25.00	$2.00	$4.00	$6.00	
	SFX: Volume I (R. Shaw)	$20.00	$3.00	$6.00	$10.00	
	SFX: Volume II (R. Abraham)	$30.00	$3.00	$6.00	$10.00	
	Film: The Lorenz System (Purchase)	$190.00	$8.00	$10.00	$15.00	
	Film: The Lorenz System (Rental)	$65.00	$8.00	$10.00	$15.00	
	Film: Chaotic Attractors of Driven Oscillators (Purchase)	$190.00	$8.00	$10.00	$15.00	
	Film: Chaotic Attractors of Driven Ocsillators (Rental)	$65.00	$8.00	$10.00	$15.00	
	Film: Strange Attractor in a Chemical System (Purchase)	$190.00	$8.00	$10.00	$15.00	
	Film: Strange Attractor in a Chemical System (Rental)	$65.00	$8.00	$10.00	$15.00	
	Zeeman BBC Videos (U-Matic)	$400.00	$12.00	$15.00	$30.00	
	Zeeman BBC Videos (VHS)	$400.00	$12.00	$15.00	$30.00	
	Crutchfield Video (U-Matic)	$65.00	$6.00	$8.00	$12.00	
	Crutchfield Video (VHS)	$65.00	$6.00	$8.00	$12.00	
	Crutchfield Video (Beta)	$65.00	$6.00	$8.00	$12.00	
	Langton Video (U-Matic)	$45.00	$6.00	$8.00	$12.00	
	Langton Video (VHS)	$45.00	$6.00	$8.00	$12.00	

☐ **Please send me your current catalog.**

CA residents add 6% Sales Tax	
TOTAL	

Name _____

Address _____

_____

City, State, Zip _____

Payment is by:

☐ Check (enclosed)

☐ Mastercard or VISA # _____ Exp. Date _____

Signature _____

Phone _____

Prices subject to change. Please call for current prices.